Puzzling Passages

In appreciation of the many
years of 'relaxed fellowship'
we have enjoyed together.

Angela

7/7/15

Puzzling Passages

John M. Hellawell

The Christadelphian
404 Shaftmoor Lane, Hall Green, Birmingham B28 8SZ, UK

2015

First published 2015

ISBN 978 0 85189 298 6 (print edition)
ISBN 978 0 85189 299 3 (electronic edition)

To Abigail and Claire

Many daughters have done well,
But you excel them all.
Proverbs 31:29 (NKJV)

Printed and bound in Malta by
Gutenberg Press Limited

Contents

Preface

THE majority of the puzzling passages considered in this book appeared in a series in *The Christadelphian* from 2005 to 2007. There were ten topics from the Old Testament and ten from the New Testament. Although these original articles have been reproduced largely unchanged, there are some fifteen new puzzling passages, also from the Old and New Testaments.

As explained in the Introduction, it is difficult to define what constitutes a puzzling passage since the 'puzzle' may simply arise from a lack of appreciation of the cultural, historical or linguistic setting of the passage. In other cases, a passage becomes a puzzle when it appears not to harmonise with other scripture.

A refutation of the unacceptable expositions of those passages that are used to support false doctrines, that is, "wrested" scriptures (2 Peter 3:16), is not provided here, since these have been comprehensively dealt with by others. It is often helpful, however, to be able, not only to demonstrate the inadequacy of these false expositions, but also to be able to provide a correct understanding, which further assists in undermining the incorrect explanations.

The topics are considered in the same order of the books and chapters of the Bible. The titles of the chapters are either quotations from scripture or, if these would be inconveniently long, a summary of the matter to be considered.

Scripture citations are mostly from the Revised Version unless indicated otherwise. References to other authors are given, usually abbreviated, in footnotes, the full citation being provided in the Bibliography.

John M. Hellawell
Peterborough
June 2015

Introduction

PUZZLING Bible passages occupy positions along a spectrum, from those which are intrinsically difficult to understand, for example 1 Corinthians 11:10, where it is said to be imperative that sisters wear head-coverings "because of the angels", to those which appear to contradict other passages or are even apparently self-contradictory, for example Proverbs 26:4,5 which at first advises us not to answer a fool according to his folly, and then to answer a fool according to his folly!

Other passages appear, at least superficially, to support the false doctrines promulgated by certain parts of Christendom. These are essentially "wrested scriptures", a topic considered by Ron Abel in his book of the same name[1] (a phrase derived from 2 Peter 3:16). A typical example is "baptism for the dead", which is practised by the Mormons on the basis of 1 Corinthians 15:29. Almost everyone, other than the Mormons, who has written about this topic, believes that their practice is invalid, but the explanations of Paul's words vary considerably and some are based on other false doctrines. Other Christadelphian writers who have dealt with wrested scriptures include Harry Whittaker[2] and Peter Watkins.[3]

This book is largely concerned with those passages that appear to be at variance with other scriptures or are simply

---

1   Abel, R. (2011[2]) *Wrested Scriptures*, The Christadelphian.
2   Whittaker, H. A. (1995) *A Look at those "Difficult" Passages*, Printland Publishers.
3   Watkins, P. (No date) *Some Difficult Passages*, 4 volumes, The Christadelphian Isolation League.

difficult to understand rather than passages that are misused in order to justify particular doctrinal positions. In the case of 1 Corinthians, cited above, the words present no serious difficulty in themselves, but are puzzling in their significance. Sometimes, the puzzle is solved by ascertaining the meaning of the words in the original Hebrew or Greek and consulting other translations. Bias by translators, as a consequence of their own beliefs, is not unknown.

Our inability to comprehend some scriptures was shared by the Apostle Peter who confessed that some of Paul's writings were "hard to be understood" (2 Peter 3:16). We must be thankful that he said they were difficult rather than impossible!

The solutions offered here may not satisfy everyone. It is evident from the literature that for some puzzles several solutions have been proposed. Sadly, certain initially attractive solutions may not survive careful scrutiny.

We can be assured, however, that "God is not the author of confusion" (1 Corinthians 14:33, KJV) and that His word has been provided for our learning that "through comfort of the scriptures we might have hope" (Romans 15:4).

Old Testament

1 |

The 'translation' of Enoch
(Genesis 5:24)

THE Genesis account in the Hebrew Old Testament of Enoch's life is brief:
"And Enoch lived sixty and five years, and begat Methuselah: and Enoch walked with God after he begat Methuselah three hundred years, and begat sons and daughters: and all the days of Enoch were three hundred sixty and five years: and Enoch walked with God: and he was not; for God took him." (Genesis 5:21-24)
There is no mention of "translation" of Enoch here; we are simply told that God "took him". The Septuagint (LXX) Greek translation of the Old Testament renders the concluding phrase by the word μετεθηκεν, *metetheken*, exactly the same word used in the Greek text of Hebrews 11:5. It is rendered as "translated" in the KJV, RV and ASV:
"By faith Enoch was translated that he should not see death; and was not found, because God had translated him: for before his translation he had this testimony, that he pleased God." (Hebrews 11:5, KJV)
Here, the writer renders "Enoch walked with God" as Enoch "pleased God", as in the LXX, and "he was not, for God took him" is given as "he was not found, because God translated him".

The term "translated"
The word "translated" is the Greek verb μετατιθημι, *metatithemi*, 'to change or remove' and "translation" is μεταθησις, *metathesis*, 'transposition, a change of position'. It is unfortunate that the

word seems to have acquired an unnecessary mystical overtone, for its other occurrences are straightforward. For example, the verb is used in Acts 7:16 where Stephen refers to the fact that the patriarchs were not buried in Egypt but some "were *carried over* into Sychem, and laid in the sepulchre that Abraham bought" (KJV) and again by Paul, who was disappointed that the Galatians were "so soon *removed* from him that called you into the grace of Christ unto another gospel" (Galatians 1:6, KJV). Earlier in Hebrews 7:12 the two words noted above are translated "being changed" and "a change": "For the priesthood *being changed* (Greek, *metatithemi*), there is made of necessity *a change* (Greek, *metathesis*) also of the law". The writer of Hebrews earlier use of these words in this way clearly indicates that to render them later as "translated" and "translation" is inconsistent and misleading.

Returning to the passage in Hebrews 11, we find that some translators add far more than the original implies. For example, at one extreme we have, "By faith Enoch was carried away to another life without passing through death" (NEB) or "Enoch was removed from this world without experiencing death" (Barclay); or again, "Enoch was taken to heaven, so that he never died" (Moffatt), a sentiment also found in the Good News Bible: "Instead, he was taken up to God ..." The direction of travel, "taken up", is also assumed in the RSV, Jerusalem Bible, NASB and the ESV. This may help explain the prevalent notion that Enoch is still alive somewhere and the most favoured location is in heaven.

Other translators avoid presuming the destination. For example, the NIV says that "Enoch was taken from this life, so that he did not experience death; he could not be found, because God had *taken him away*". This version avoids the implication that Enoch went to heaven, but still suggests that he did not die.

The New Testament, in at least two places, provides evidence of what happened to Enoch. First, the letter to the Hebrews affirms that Enoch did die. After reviewing the faithful examples of Abel, Enoch, Noah and Abraham the writer adds, "These *all* died in faith, not having received the promises"

(Hebrews 11:13). Second, we have John's clear declaration: "And *no man* hath ascended up to heaven" (John 3:13, KJV).

Given this New Testament commentary, we may now return to the Genesis record, noting that it gives no indication of his "translation", as is commonly understood, but provides genealogical information, repeated emphasis of his walking with God and ending with the enigmatic, "and he was not, for God took him". The phrase, "walked with God" is also used of Noah (Genesis 6:9), who is described as "righteous" and "perfect" (or "upright", KJV margin or "blameless", RV margin), attributes which, one may infer, were shared by Enoch.

An early death?

It must be noted that the text clearly says, "*all* the days of Enoch were three hundred sixty and five years" indicating the actual life-span of this godly man. We may be concerned that a man of such faith lived for less than half the years of his predecessors and descendants, but it may be that there were reasons for this. Knowing as we do, that death is an unconscious state, it may well have been in God's mercy that he died relatively young, for reasons which are discussed below. The time from his death to the resurrection would, for him, pass as with all saints, as "a moment ... the twinkling of an eye".

What is significant is that, for all the other individuals in Genesis 5, their lives end with the phrase "and he died", while for Enoch the phrase is, "and he was not; for God took him". This difference may also have contributed to the mystique surrounding Enoch, yet a little work with a concordance will reveal that the phrase "was not" is "a poetic euphemism for death".[1] Examples include the inadvertent references by Reuben and his brothers regarding Joseph: "And he returned unto his brethren, and said, The child *is not*; and I, whither shall I go?" (Genesis 37:30); "And they said, We thy servants are twelve brethren, the sons of one man in the land of Canaan; and, behold, the youngest is this

---

1   Wenham, G. J. (1987) Genesis 1-15, *Word Biblical Commentary*, page 128.

day with our father, and one *is not*" (42:13); and "We be twelve brethren, sons of our father; one *is not*, and the youngest is this day with our father in the land of Canaan" (verse 32). Similarly, we might add Jeremiah 31:15 (and its New Testament citation): "Thus saith the LORD; A voice is heard in Ramah, lamentation, and bitter weeping, Rachel weeping for her children; she refuseth to be comforted for her children, because they *are not*"; and Lamentations 5:7: "Our fathers have sinned, and *are not*; and we have borne their iniquities."

The respected Hebrew scholar Cassuto states that the intention of the text "is not to convey that Enoch did not die (it is written: and he was not!), but only that his death was not like the death of other people ..."[2] What may be significant between the phrases "and he died" and "he was not" is the manner of death. The former may refer to a natural death, when the family has a body which they are able to bury, while the latter may indicate a presumed death, as would be the case with Jacob and Joseph, without a body and therefore without a burial. In Jeremiah's prophecy, the Babylonian destruction of Jerusalem involved burning it (Jeremiah 32:28,29) which would prevent a normal burial. The "massacre of the innocents" (Matthew 2:16) might also have involved such a mass butchery that identification of the children would prevent a normal burial.

Thus, the Genesis account indicates that Enoch died and also God took him. This may be a reference to his removal physically in order that he should not "see death", as in Hebrews, or that his death was the result of divine intervention. Combining the Genesis and Hebrews accounts, it would seem that Enoch was exceptionally spiritual and, if he was outspoken against the wickedness of his contemporaries, in danger of a premature and probably violent death. Hebrews 11 therefore explains that Enoch "was not *found*" (verse 5), suggesting that God removed him to a safe location away from his enemies, where he ended his days at a relatively young age for an antediluvian patriarch.

---

2   Cassuto, U. (1961) *A Commentary on the Book of Genesis, Part One*, page 286.

A wicked world

Finally, we must consider why Enoch was "translated", so that he should not see death, and whether scripture gives any hint as to the reason. The circumstances under which Enoch lived may be significant. The brief account of his life is contained within the "book of the generations of Adam" in Genesis 5, which follows the boasting of Lamech of the line of Cain (4:23), and a statement that, "then began men to call upon the name of the LORD", implying that these men were in the line of Seth. In the next chapter we have the Lord stating that His spirit would not always strive with man (6:3) and that "the wickedness of man was great in the earth, and that every imagination of the thoughts of his heart was only evil continually". The situation became beyond recovery and the Flood destroyed that evil population. Given this context, is it probable that Enoch, of whom we are told twice that he "walked with God", was physically removed to prevent an even more premature and violent death at the hands of his wicked contemporaries? The New Testament indicates that Enoch warned them of coming divine judgement:

"And to these also Enoch, the seventh from Adam, prophesied, saying, Behold, the Lord came with ten thousands of his holy ones, to execute judgment upon all, and to convict all the ungodly of all their works of ungodliness which they have ungodly wrought, and of all the hard things which ungodly sinners have spoken against him."   (Jude 14,15)

This denouncement would have placed him in danger of losing his life and removal to a safer location would have prevented this.

There are other examples elsewhere in scripture of someone being carried away into the air to arrive at another location, including Elijah (1 Kings 18:12; 2 Kings 2:16) and Philip (Acts 8:39). It seems that there will be another, literal mass "translation" at the Lord's return (1 Thessalonians 4:17).

SUMMARY

Enoch died (Hebrews 11:13) aged 365 (Genesis 5:23) and the Hebrew phrase "was not" indicates death. The word "translation"

(Hebrews 11:5) in the Greek text is the normal word for removal. Enoch's 'translation' was simply a removal elsewhere, probably in order to prevent his suffering a violent death. He did not ascend to heaven (John 3:13).

The sons of God and the daughters of men
(Genesis 6:2)

T HE puzzle in this passage concerns the identity of the "sons of God" and the "daughters of men". Who, then, were these "sons of God"? The standard Jewish explanation is that they were angels. This idea was, no doubt, derived from passages where the phrase seems to describe the angels, for Job refers to creation when "the morning stars sang together, and all the sons of God shouted for joy" (Job 38:7). The NIV quite reasonably translates this as "angels". Rabbinical exposition asserts that confirmation of this view is seen in the consequences of the union of angels and women: "mighty men ... men of renown" were born to them. Some commentators equate these "sons of God" with the 'fallen angels' of 2 Peter 2:4 and Jude 6. We can dismiss this fanciful explanation quite readily on the authority of the Lord Jesus, who declared that the angels "neither marry, nor are given in marriage" (Mark 12:25; Luke 20:35,36).

An evil age
In subsequent verses we have the Lord indicating that His Spirit will not contend with man for ever (Genesis 6:3); that He saw how great mankind's wickedness on the earth had become because every inclination of the thoughts of their hearts was only evil all the time (verse 5) and He was grieved that He had made man on the earth, and His heart was filled with pain (verse 6). The final stage was the decision by the Lord to destroy mankind (verse 7) because of the unmitigated corruption and violence in the earth

(verses 11,12), by means of a cataclysmic flood (verse 17). These circumstances are set in marked contrast with the life of Noah:

"These are the generations of Noah. Noah was a righteous man, and perfect in his generations: Noah walked with God ... Thus did Noah; according to all that God commanded him, so did he."   (Genesis 6:9,22)

"And the LORD said unto Noah, Come thou and all thy house into the ark; for thee have I seen righteous before me in this generation."   (Genesis 7:1)

Since the passage under consideration comes immediately before these descriptions of the shocking prevailing conditions, for which God's drastic solution was to send the flood, and immediately after the genealogy of Noah, we may reasonably assume that verse 2 is not simply a passing comment but an integral part of this section of scripture. Any exegesis of this passage must be consonant with the condition of the world at this time.

The common assumption is that the "sons of God" are the godly line and "the daughters of men" are the worldly population. This would be an early example of 'marrying out of the Truth', and might appear attractive at first sight, but this hardly fits the context above. It is significant that the text does not mention any marriage arrangements but only that these sons of God "took them wives of all that they chose". It is quite possible that this indicates violent abduction. The phrase "wives of all that they chose" also implies polygamy and the basis of their selection was that these daughters of men were "fair" (*beautiful* NIV; *attractive* ESV): that is, they were physically attractive but not necessarily godly (see below). If this assessment is correct, it is in accord with the description of the antediluvian world.

Alternative translations

The original Hebrew phrase, here translated "sons of God", is rendered differently in other places in the Old Testament. The "of God" part of the phrase can serve as a strong adjective meaning 'mighty'. There are examples of this in Genesis at chapter 1:2

where "Spirit of God" has been rendered as "mighty wind" (NEB), and at chapter 23:6 where Abraham is described by the sons of Heth as a "mighty prince", which the KJV margin gives as "Heb., 'a prince of God'".

Elsewhere, the Hebrew phrase *b^ene-ha'elohim*, 'sons of God', is rendered "mighty ones" or "sons of the mighty". For example, in Psalm 29:1 it is "ye mighty" (KJV), "sons of the mighty" (RV margin / ASV), "mighty ones" (NIV). Similarly, in Psalm 89:6 it is translated "sons of the mighty" (KJV / RV / ASV). The RV margin of Psalm 58:1 gives as an alternative, "Or, as otherwise read, 'O ye gods' or, 'O ye mighty ones'", indicating that the Hebrew is capable of both meanings.

The example of Lamech?

If this is a legitimate alternative translation in Genesis 6:2 then we may have a solution to our puzzle. It is significant that the Samaritan Pentateuch has "sons of the mighty" rather than "sons of God" in this passage.

The mention of "giants" in verse 4 (KJV) may also relate to the violence of the age. The Hebrew word is *Nephilim*,[1] which may derive from the root 'to fell',[2] again suggesting violence. It is only found here and Numbers 13:33, where the spies reported that the men they encountered were tall, and this may have determined the translation "giants". Looking again at Genesis 6:2, as noted above, one gains the impression that "took ... all that they chose"[3] is a description of abduction rather than consent and also implies that they acquired more than one wife by this process.

The male children of the forced union of the evil "sons of the mighty" and the abducted "daughters of men" were "mighty men ... of old, the men of renown". Perhaps the phrase "mighty

---

1   The word for giants elsewhere is Rephaim. Nephilim is from the root *naphal*, to fall, to make to fall, to fell.

2   The word also is found in 2 Kings 3:19, ASV: "And ye shall ... fell (cut down, NIV) every good tree."

3   NIV has "any of them they chose".

men ... of old" indicated that they patterned themselves on the model of Lamech who boasted that he was quite capable of defending himself and nobody would dare trifle with him (Genesis 4:23,24), especially since his son appeared to have the metallurgical capability to construct weapons.

It may be that these men are referred to in the book of Job: "Hast thou marked the old way which wicked men have trodden? which were cut down out of time, whose foundation was overflown with a flood: which said unto God, Depart from us: and what can the Almighty do for them [to us, RV margin]."
(Job 22:15-17, KJV)

Jude may also be alluding to them:
"And to these also Enoch, the seventh from Adam, prophesied, saying, Behold, the Lord came with ten thousands of his holy ones, to execute judgment upon all, and to convict all the ungodly of all their works of ungodliness which they have ungodly wrought, and of all the hard things which ungodly sinners have spoken against him."   (Jude 14,15)

A preacher of righteousness

God did not act speedily to destroy the wicked but provided witness against them through Noah, a preacher of righteousness, for a considerable period during which they had opportunity to repent. The duration of this anarchy can be deduced from the lifespan of Noah. As he lived for 350 years after the flood (Genesis 9:28) and his total lifespan was 950 (verse 29), he must have lived for almost 600 years before the flood came.

This accords with Peter's comment about God's longsuffering (literally 'patience', μακροθυμια *macrothumia*) with those whom He finally destroyed with the flood:
"... that aforetime were disobedient, when the longsuffering of God waited in the days of Noah, while the ark was a preparing, wherein few, that is, eight souls, were saved through water."
(1 Peter 3:20)

We too can be grateful that this characteristic is still an aspect of God's name and nature (Exodus 34:6,7; 2 Peter 3:9,15).

SUMMARY

The "sons of God" can be translated "the sons of the mighty". They are the ungodly, characterised by their use of force in abducting the "daughters of men" who belong to more peaceful families. The contemporary scene is one in which sin and violence increased, and spirituality decreased, to such an extent that ultimately the whole population, except for eight, was destroyed by the flood.

"I and the lad will ... come again to you"
(Genesis 22:5)

THE puzzle in this familiar passage is superficially one of omission although, as we shall see, what we are not told may be highly significant. The offering of Isaac is a key episode in redemptive history. James not only emphasises the tangible expression of Abraham's faith in offering up Isaac, but also that it was the fulfilment of a scripture which had declared that his faith was imputed to him for righteousness:

"Was not Abraham our father justified by works, in that he offered up Isaac his son upon the altar? Thou seest that faith wrought with his works, and by works was faith made perfect; and the scripture was fulfilled which saith, And Abraham believed God, and it was reckoned unto him for righteousness; and he was called the friend of God." (James 2:21-23)

In addition, Paul tells us that this scripture "was not written for his sake alone, that it was reckoned unto him ..." (Romans 4:23), indicating not only that it existed in Abraham's day, written for his sake, but "for our sake also, unto whom it shall be reckoned, who believe on him that raised Jesus our Lord from the dead" (verse 24).

"In Isaac shall thy seed be called"
The account in Genesis 22 begins with the testing of Abraham. The divine command was clear:

"Take now thy son, thine only son, whom thou lovest, even Isaac, and get thee into the land of Moriah; and offer him there for a burnt offering upon one of the mountains which I will tell thee of." (Genesis 22:2)

This godly man had waited twenty-five years for the birth of his only son by Sarah; the son whom he loved dearly and the son he named 'laughter' because of the joy he brought him (Genesis 17:17). More than this, Abraham had been told, "In Isaac shall thy seed be called" (21:12). This was, of course, more than a promise of progeny: this was the line through which the Redeemer should come.

Now he was being commanded, not only to slay Isaac and bring the line of the seed to an end, but also to offer him as a burnt offering! Yet God had never required human sacrifice; indeed it would be offensive to Him.

Here was a dilemma indeed: if Abraham obeyed how would the promised seed come? Again, how could a man of such great faith disobey God? The dilemma could only be resolved if Isaac was the promised Redeemer! The writer of Hebrews explains that this is exactly what Abraham concluded:

"By faith Abraham, being tried, offered up Isaac: yea, he that had gladly received the promises was offering up his only begotten son; even he to whom it was said, In Isaac shall thy seed be called: accounting that God is able to raise up, even from the dead; from whence he did also in a parable receive him back." (Hebrews 11:17,18)

Isaac was not killed, but the 'stay of execution' was effectively a resurrection prefiguring that of the true "seed, which is Christ" (Galatians 3:16). So many aspects of this episode anticipate the experiences of the Lord Jesus. For example, the involvement of an only son and two others, the wood laid on Isaac, Isaac's willing submission and the location is the same, for Moriah is Jerusalem (2 Chronicles 3:1).

As Abraham left the two young men, he indicated that he and Isaac would return:

"Abide ye here with the ass, and I and the lad will go yonder; and we will worship, and come again to you." (Genesis 22:5)

After receiving the seventh and final promise, in which Abraham was assured that in his seed all the nations of the earth would be blessed and God swore by Himself when he made that promise, is it merely coincidence that afterwards Abraham went, with his servants, to live at Beer-sheba, the 'well of the oath'?

The record continues:

"So Abraham returned unto his young men, and they rose up and went together to Beer-sheba; and Abraham dwelt at Beer-sheba."   (Genesis 22:19)

There is no mention of Isaac! Are we to assume that he returned with Abraham even though there is no mention of his presence? Or is this omission significant? Experience has taught us that God's word has meticulousness unlike other writings and every detail is significant. This view is confirmed by the way in which the Lord Jesus relied on a word or even the tense of a verb in his arguments with opponents.[1]

"Which things are an allegory"

Where was Isaac? If we turn over the pages of Genesis we next meet him in 24:62 having returned to Hebron[2] from Beer lahai-roi. The name of this well is said to mean 'the well of living after seeing'.[3] Again we have an interesting link with the events in Mount Moriah. Abraham named the place Jehovah-jireh (Genesis 22:14, RV margin, "That is, *The* LORD *will see,* or *provide*") and Isaac came from Beer lahai-roi, 'the well of living after seeing' – another allusion to his figurative resurrection.

Much is recorded between Isaac's 'disappearance' from the record at Moriah and his reappearance at Hebron. Abraham's servant had been sent to acquire a wife for Abraham's only son and she left her kin willingly (24:58) in order to join one whom she had not seen.

---

1   See, for example, John 10:34-36 citing Psalm 82:6, and Matthew 22:32 citing Exodus 3:6.
2   Isaac brought Rebekah to his mother Sarah's tent which was last located at Hebron (Genesis 23:2).
3   See note by Bullinger, *The Companion Bible,* on Genesis 16:13,14.

There is surely significance in Isaac's figurative sacrifice, his absence and his reappearance to take his bride. Could this be amongst the things "which are an allegory", like the relationship between Sarah and Hagar (Galatians 4:24) and the status of Melchizedek (Hebrews 7:2,3)? Without the guidance of the inspired writers would we have recognised these allegories?

This puzzle started from a very small problem: a simple omission which could easily be overlooked and yet which seems to have been deliberate in order to add to the very certain parallels between Isaac and the Lord Jesus. One cannot help but wonder what else we might have missed!

SUMMARY

The divine command to sacrifice Isaac would present Abraham with a paradox, for the promises were dependent on Isaac having at least one son in the line of the seed: "In Isaac shall thy seed be called." In Hebrews 11:19 we learn that Abraham expected his son to be resurrected and, in a sense he was. One would assume that this is why Abraham was willing to sacrifice his son: he thought Isaac was the promised Messiah. This is also why Abraham explained to his two servants that after he and Isaac had worshipped they would both return, but there is no record that Isaac did. In all probability he did return with Abraham but the omission is significant, and similar to that regarding the ancestry of Melchizedek where what is not revealed is as important as what is. Isaac 'disappears' from the record for over ninety verses, but the next time he appears it is to meet and marry his bride! Here we have an allegory of redemptive history: the only son, who is sacrificed and raised, goes away and returns to take his bride.

The sons of Keturah
(Genesis 25:1-5)

A T the opening of Genesis 25 we read the following information about Abraham and some of his descendants:

"Abraham took another wife, whose name was Keturah. She bore him Zimran, Jokshan, Medan, Midian, Ishbak and Shuah. Jokshan was the father of Sheba and Dedan; the descendants of Dedan were the Asshurites, the Letushites and the Leummites. The sons of Midian were Ephah, Epher, Hanoch, Abida and Eldaah. All these were descendants of Keturah. Abraham left everything he owned to Isaac."

(Genesis 25:1-5, NIV)

"With God all things are possible"
As the death of Sarah is recorded at the beginning of chapter 23 we might suppose that Abraham married Keturah after Sarah's death. This would not be a puzzle were it not for the New Testament comments regarding the improbability, if not impossibility, of Abraham having a son when aged 100. Paul, writing in Romans, says:

"Against all hope, Abraham in hope believed and so became the father of many nations, just as it had been said to him, 'So shall your offspring be.' Without weakening in his faith, he faced the fact that his body was as good as dead – since he was about a hundred years old – and that Sarah's womb was also dead. Yet he did not waver through unbelief regarding the promise of God, but was strengthened in his faith and gave glory to God, being fully persuaded that God had power to do what he had promised."   (Romans 4:18-21, NIV) Paul stresses the improbability of Abraham fathering a son and also the impossibility that Sarah could conceive. We are told in Genesis 18: "Abraham and Sarah were already old and well advanced in years, and Sarah was past the age of childbearing" (Genesis 18:11, NIV).

The last phrase is rather euphemistic in the NIV. The KJV and RV render it more specifically, it had "ceased to be with Sarah after the manner of women". We are to conclude, therefore, that the conception of Isaac was virtually impossible from a medical standpoint. This is the essence of Paul's argument regarding the quality of Abraham's faith: he believed in the impossible because God, with whom all things are possible, had promised it. This is endorsed by the writer of Hebrews:

"By faith Abraham, even though he was past age – and Sarah herself was barren – was enabled to become a father because he considered him faithful who had made the promise. And so from this one man, and he as good as dead, came descendants as numerous as the stars in the sky and as countless as the sand on the seashore."   (Hebrews 11:11,12, NIV)

Given these clear New Testament comments we may wonder why great store is placed on Abraham fathering a child when aged 100 (Genesis 17:17; 21:5), yet nothing remarkable is said about the birth of a further six sons when, apparently at the age of about 140, he took Keturah.

Some commentators have suggested that Abraham was rejuvenated in his old age and this explains the birth of a further six sons. While this is a possibility, it seems contrary to the spirit of the comments in Romans and Hebrews. An alternative explanation is that the Genesis text at this point is not strictly chronological, a conclusion shared by many commentators.

"Abraham had taken another wife ..."

A simple solution is given by the marginal comment of the NIV, and expanded in the NIV Study Bible notes, where it is said that the text could be translated "had taken", indicating that this had occurred at some time in the past and not subsequent to the events of Genesis 24. Evidence that the text may not be chronological at this point is found elsewhere. For example, we have Abraham's steward explaining to Laban and Bethuel that Abraham had already given everything to Isaac in Genesis 24:36, while we are first told this in the narrative in the next chapter (25:5).

In Genesis 25:6 we are told that the sons of the concubines (plural) were sent away eastward. We only know of Hagar, though she is not specifically called a concubine anywhere but a "handmaid" (see RV). Keturah is called a "wife" in 25:1, but in 1 Chronicles 1:32 she is said to be a "concubine" and her sons are listed. This is, presumably, her true status. It may be that, when this part of the Genesis record was written, Sarah had died and Hagar had been sent away with Ishmael, so that the only one left was Keturah who would now be reckoned as a "wife". The strange comment that Abraham gave gifts to the sons of the concubines and sent them away from Isaac his son eastward "while he yet lived" (Genesis 25:6), may also indicate that this occurred some considerable time earlier since Abraham's lifespan and death are recorded in the next two verses (7,8).

The sequence of the genealogies in 1 Chronicles 1, although by no means conclusive, does suggest that Keturah's sons were born before Isaac was conceived.[1] The order is: sons of Ishmael (verses 29-31); sons of Keturah (verses 32,33) and then, "And Abraham begat Isaac. The sons of Isaac; Esau and Israel" (verse 34).

Finally, we may reasonably ask why Abraham would remarry after the death of Sarah and the birth of the promised seed so late in his life. The record of Sarah's death is quite moving:

"Sarah lived to be a hundred and twenty-seven years old. She died at Kiriath Arba (that is, Hebron) in the land of Canaan, and

---

1   See Lewis, R. (2014) *Abraham & Sarah*, Appendix 4, page 221, where the same conclusion is reached.

Abraham went to mourn for Sarah and to weep over her."
(Genesis 23:1,2, NIV)

His care in securing a grave for Sarah, which became the family vault[2] in the cave at Machpelah, bought at extortionate cost,[3] was highly significant for one who had been promised the whole land.

SUMMARY

In Romans and Hebrews attention is drawn to the great age at which Abraham fathered Isaac, yet Genesis 25 lists a further six sons born to Abraham and Keturah apparently after Sarah's death. The account in 1 Chronicles 1 suggests that these sons were born after Ishmael and before Isaac.

---

2   This vault ultimately held Isaac, Sarah, Rebekah, Abraham and Leah. Is it a coincidence that the first letters of their names spell 'Israel' (in Hebrew), the name of the other occupant of this tomb? See Whittaker, H. A. (1989[2]) *Abraham, Father of the Faithful*, page 101.

3   David bought the threshing-floor of Araunah the Jebusite for fifty shekels of silver (2 Samuel 24:24) some thousand years later!

The deception perpetrated on Isaac
(Genesis 27)

T HE episode described in Genesis 27, where Rebekah persuaded Jacob to impersonate his brother in order to obtain the blessing of the firstborn, poses several problems. Firstly, why did Isaac intend to bless Esau and not Jacob when, as we shall see, it was God's intention that Jacob would have pre-eminence? Secondly, why did Rebekah and Jacob feel that they had to perpetrate the deception rather than confront Isaac? Was Isaac no longer a man of faith? Earlier he had been compliant to God's will when he was about to be sacrificed by Abraham. He received a divine blessing similar to those which his father obtained (Genesis 26:2-5,24), and his experiences in Philistine territory with respect to Rebekah were parallel with those of Abraham (Genesis 20) with reference to Sarah. However, later we see his willingness to make an alliance with Abimelech and he allows Esau to marry the daughters of Hittites, knowing full well his father's concern that his own wife should not be taken "of the daughters of the Canaanites".

"Two nations are in thy womb"
In order to try to solve the puzzles we need to go back to chapter 25 where the failure of Rebekah to conceive is recorded (verse 21). Isaac was forty when he married Rebekah and he was sixty when Esau and Jacob were born (verse 26). So, for twenty years they were a childless couple. This would be a trial under any circumstances, but when your family is the beneficiary of divine promises regarding descendants who would become

innumerable, and a seed in whom all the nations of the earth were to be blessed, then a barren wife in that direct line would be difficult to understand. An additional problem for Isaac would be the knowledge that his father Abraham had gone to great lengths to ensure that Isaac's wife was chosen from their kindred (chapter 24). The remarkable experiences related by Abraham's eldest servant (probably Eliezer of Damascus, Genesis 15:2) on his return with Isaac's bride-to-be would indicate that the hand of God was evident in all that had happened.

After twenty years of disappointment, the prayers of Isaac were answered and Rebekah became pregnant. The discomforts sometimes experienced by expectant mothers became so intense that Rebekah went to enquire of the Lord the reason for her condition. We might wonder where she went. It may be that she went to Melchizedek or even to Abraham, for he was a prophet (Genesis 20:7; Psalm 105:15) and lived until Esau and Jacob were fifteen years old. The answer was:

> "Two nations are in thy womb, and two peoples shall be separated even from thy bowels: and the one people shall be stronger than the other people; and the elder shall serve the younger."   (Genesis 25:23)

For our present purpose, the concluding statement, "and the elder shall serve the younger", is the most significant. This was the divine decree and one would assume that Rebekah informed Isaac of this.

Two different characters

In due course the twin boys were born and Esau was the elder. As they grew their characters were quite different: Esau was a skilled hunter and a man of the outdoors while Jacob was a "plain man" living in tents. The word translated "plain" is capable of a variety of meanings as a glance at a selection of Bible versions will reveal. For example, we have "quiet" (RSV, NIV), "peaceful" (NASB), "mild" (NKJV), "homely" (Darby). The NEB says Jacob "led a settled life", contrasting with Esau as "a man of the open plains". It is evident from usages elsewhere (e.g., 6:9, with reference to

Noah; Job 1:1,8) that it means 'upright', 'perfect', or 'undefiled'. This is endorsed by the comment in Hebrews 12:16 regarding the behaviour of Esau, which included immorality and profanity.

The following comment is probably the key to understanding the circumstances which led ultimately to the need for the deception:

> "Now Isaac loved Esau, because he did eat of his venison: and Rebekah loved Jacob."   (Genesis 25:28)

The division of parental affections was a recipe for disaster. Isaac probably admired the son who fulfilled his own frustrated ambitions and there was, of course, the venison which, no doubt, made a welcome change from lamb or mutton! Rebekah loved the son who accepted his responsibilities for the family enterprise and, unlike Esau, was devoted to spiritual matters.

On one of the occasions when Esau returned from a hunting trip empty-handed, Jacob seized the opportunity to formalise what he knew was God's intention, namely that he should inherit the blessings of the firstborn. Esau was faint with hunger and Jacob was cooking a meal in a pot, probably a stew made with lentils which imparted the red colour. In response to the request from Esau for a portion of the stew, Jacob suggested that Esau should pay for it with his birthright. Esau replied that, as he was likely to die, presumably he meant prematurely as a result of his lifestyle, the birthright was of no value to him and so he readily sold it for "one mess of meat" (Hebrews 12:16). It is not certain that Isaac and Rebekah were aware of this transaction.

Isaac's determination to bless Esau

As Isaac advanced in years, his eyesight deteriorated to the point of blindness and he began to contemplate the prospect of his death. Calling Esau, Isaac asked him to hunt venison and cook the savoury meal which he enjoyed so much. After the meal, Isaac would impart the patriarchal blessing of the firstborn on Esau. Whether Isaac's memory had also begun to fail, or he had decided to ignore the information imparted when Rebekah enquired of the Lord, is not clear. We may have to accept the possibility that Rebekah kept this to herself, but it seems highly unlikely given the fact that the prediction included the birth of twins – information that would have gladdened Isaac's heart given that he waited for twenty years without a child and then was granted two sons. Isaac's behaviour seems to indicate that his faith was waning. He had not grown spiritually, and living in proximity to the Philistines and related by marriage to the Hittites, his attitude had become worldly. He preferred to favour his profane son, a-man-of-the-world in the very worst sense, rather than the upright and spiritual son.

Rebekah was evidently a godly woman and, when she overheard the conversation between Isaac and Esau, she immediately resolved to frustrate Isaac and ensure that Jacob obtained the blessing of the firstborn which was his by divine decree and also by commercial transaction. It is surely significant that she did not simply confront Isaac with her concerns: perhaps she knew that he would not listen to reason and that she would have to use other means to foil him.

The importance of such a blessing can hardly be overemphasised. The patriarchal blessings are far more than pious wishes for the success of the next, and succeeding, generations. These blessings are solemn announcements which have a strong prophetic component and, it seems, once uttered cannot be altered. Although this is not explicitly stated, it would appear that they are given under divine inspiration and, therefore, indicate God's intentions for the future of the chosen line.

Rebekah resolved to cook some savoury food for Isaac and arrange for Jacob to take it to his father and obtain the blessing before Esau returned from hunting venison. When she explained her plan to Jacob, he realised that the subterfuge would not work: the physical characteristics of his brother were so different that even the blindness of Isaac would not conceal his true identity. Again, we may wonder why Jacob did not confront his father and claim the blessing that was rightfully his, reminding him of the divine edict and also the purchase of the birthright. His apparent reluctance to do so tends to suggest that Rebekah's assessment of the intransigence of Isaac was correct.

Jacob was concerned that if the deception failed he would receive a curse and not a blessing. Rebekah responded by saying that she would accept responsibility for failure and any consequential curse. So, Jacob complied and two good kids of the flock were slaughtered to provide the meat for the savoury meal and skins to simulate Esau's prolific hairiness. The skins were made into gloves for Jacob's hands and wrists and a scarf to cover his smooth neck. Jacob donned the "goodly raiment" of Esau, possibly a special garment of the firstborn, and carried the savoury meat and bread into his father.

"I am Esau thy firstborn"

Jacob announced his arrival and Isaac asked who he was. Perhaps Isaac had not expected a visit from anyone other than Esau and the voice that he heard was not Esau's. Jacob replied:

"I am Esau thy firstborn; I have done according as thou badest me: arise, I pray thee, sit and eat of my venison, that thy soul may bless me." (Genesis 27:19)

The reply should have reassured Isaac. His discourse with Esau had been confidential and only he would have known that Isaac had asked for the savoury meat before he was to impart the blessing. Yet it seems that Isaac was still suspicious. He asked how it was that he had been able to find a deer so quickly, knowing that it normally took quite a while to locate one and succeed in a kill. Jacob's instinctive reply intensified Isaac's concern: "Because the LORD thy God sent me good speed" (verse 20). We may imagine that this was not the kind of answer Esau would give. More likely he would have claimed that it was the result of his hunting prowess.

Isaac was concerned to check the identity of the one who was claiming to be his firstborn by his sense of touch. Isaac asked that he should come close in order that the true identity could be ascertained. The dilemma was not resolved, for Isaac exclaimed that the voice was Jacob's but the hands were Esau's. So Isaac asked again, Are you really my son Esau? Jacob lied once more and affirmed that he was Esau.

Perhaps by now the smell of the savoury meal was having its effect and Isaac finally accepted the assurance that his companion was indeed Esau. After he had dined and wined, Isaac asked that his son should come and kiss him. The close proximity enabled Isaac to smell the odour of the "goodly raiment" which possibly had been anointed and so was quite distinctive. Isaac was now reassured and proceeded to declare the patriarchal blessing:

> "And God give thee of the dew of heaven, and of the fatness of the earth, and plenty of corn and wine: let peoples serve thee, and nations bow down to thee: be lord over thy brethren, and let thy mother's sons bow down to thee: cursed be every one that curseth thee, and blessed be every one that blesseth thee."   (Genesis 27:28,29)

The blessing contains elements similar to those given to Abraham and to Isaac himself but, in general, the tone is materialistic rather than spiritual.

"Isaac trembled very exceedingly"

No sooner had Jacob left his father's presence than Esau returned. When offered the savoury meat, Isaac became alarmed and demanded that the visitor identify himself. When he received the reply that he was Esau, his firstborn son, Isaac began to tremble "very exceedingly". The KJV margin gives the literal Hebrew as "trembled with a great trembling greatly".

He asked again who his visitor was but, without waiting for the reply, he then asked who it was that had brought the savoury meat and had received the blessing. Then, in a flash he realised who it was and what he had done. Isaac trembled because he had thought to foil God's purpose and now he found himself thwarted. His conclusion said it all: "Yea, and he shall be blessed" (verse 33).

God had declared: "And the elder shall serve the younger" and nothing could change this. The deception may have been wrong in principle and Jacob's lies cannot be overlooked, but God's purpose was achieved. While we may feel that Rebekah's scheme of deception and Jacob's complicity and lies cannot be condoned, it is surely significant that there is no scriptural condemnation of what transpired. One may speculate what might have happened had Rebekah not intervened but the outcome would have been the same: Jacob would receive the blessing. Here is an important lesson: we can work with God or we can rebel, but we cannot frustrate God's intentions.

"Esau lifted up his voice, and wept"

Esau now insisted that he should be blessed, protesting that Jacob was well-named "supplanter" for he had done this twice, first with the birthright and now with the blessing. Isaac could not withdraw the blessing even if Esau was now in tears. The comment in Hebrews is apposite:

> "For ye know that even when he afterward desired to inherit the blessing, he was rejected; for he found no place for a change of mind in his father, though he sought it diligently with tears."   (Hebrews 12:17, ASV)

There was no possibility of Isaac changing his mind. At last he had conceded that God's decision was right. Yet he could predict what would happen to Esau:

> "... Behold, of the fatness of the earth shall be thy dwelling, and of the dew of heaven from above; and by thy sword shalt thou live, and thou shalt serve thy brother; and it shall come to pass when thou shalt break loose, that thou shalt shake his yoke from off thy neck."   (Genesis 27:39,40)

The passage appears to suggest that Esau would live with the "fatness of the earth", but the preposition 'of' may also be 'from' or 'away from' as in the following translation:

> "Your dwelling will be away from the earth's richness, away from the dew of heaven above. You will live by the sword and you will serve your brother. But when you grow restless, you will throw his yoke from off your neck."   (Genesis 27:39,40, NIV)

This matches the subsequent history of Esau, that is, Edom most accurately, as we should expect. Two brothers, who had so little in common, were soon to part company. Esau's jealousy had resulted in a plan to murder his brother once their father had died. Once more, Rebekah was to bring her motherly concern to bear in devising a scheme to protect her favourite son.

The two nations that began their struggle in Rebekah's womb are still in conflict and this will not be resolved until the One who is the principal subject of the patriarchal blessings returns to fulfil them.

SUMMARY

The ethical problems posed by the deception that Rebekah perpetrated, with the connivance of Jacob in impersonating his brother and also lying, can only be excused by the fact that their motivation was to secure the previously expressed divine intention that Esau, although the firstborn, would be replaced by Jacob. The behaviour of Isaac is also problematic in that he must have known God's intention and he certainly acknowledged it when he realised that he could not frustrate God's purpose. While Rebekah and Jacob failed to show faith in God's ability to secure His purpose unaided, they were instrumental in attaining His purpose and it should be noted that there is no condemnation of their behaviour in scripture.

The Ethiopian wife of Moses
(Numbers 12:1)

T HE incident of the Cushite or Ethiopian wife of Moses in Numbers 12 appears suddenly and without explanation. It is evident that Moses' marriage had occurred sometime earlier, yet there is no record in scripture. Equally puzzling is the reaction of Aaron and Miriam, as recorded at the beginning of Numbers chapter 12:

"And Miriam and Aaron spake against Moses because of the Cushite woman whom he had married: for he had married a Cushite woman." (verse 1)

Again, the record does not give any indication as to why this incident is mentioned. Was it because she had appeared unexpectedly in the camp in the wilderness?

Jealous of Moses?
We know that Moses already had a wife. He had married Zipporah, one of the seven daughters of Reuel – also called Jethro and Raguel – the priest of Midian (Exodus 2:16-21; 3:1; Numbers 10:29). She was the mother of his sons Gershom and Eliezer. Midian was one of the sons of Abraham by Keturah (Genesis 25:2). Moses was, therefore, a distant relative of Reuel, who almost certainly worshipped the Lord.

It is evident that this Cushite wife was in addition to Zipporah. The actual cause of the resentment on the part of Aaron and Miriam is not specified. It seems unlikely that it was because of 'bigamy', for the law made provision for two wives. It has been suggested that this was essentially a case of racial discrimination, possibly on the grounds of colour since Ethiopians (perhaps more accurately Nubians) were dark-skinned. It is possible that Aaron and Miriam were concerned for Gershom and Eliezer since there could be children by this Cushite woman.

Some commentators have suggested that the appearance of the Cushite wife was not the actual reason for complaint but rather was used as an excuse to attack Moses. Perhaps jealousy of Moses had simmered beneath the surface for some time and this incident, hardly significant in itself, became the catalyst for the outburst.

The criticism of Moses by Aaron and Miriam concerned his status. They implied that he had become conceited and was too full of himself. Were they not just as important as he was? "Hath [the LORD] not spoken also with us?" (Numbers 12:2).

Meek above all men

The text sets the record straight:

> "Now the man Moses was very meek, above all the men which
> were upon the face of the earth."   (verse 3)

There was no hint that Moses thought too highly of himself: the accusation was totally unjustified. In addition, the severe reaction of the Lord vindicated Moses. Calling Moses, Aaron and Miriam to the tabernacle, the Lord reminded Aaron and Miriam of the unique status of Moses. Other prophets would be informed by visions or dreams but, for his faithfulness, Moses was privileged to converse directly with the angel of the Lord.

The Lord's angel departed and Miriam was inflicted with leprosy. One cannot help but wonder whether this was because she was the instigator of the complaint,[1] disapproving of this foreigner who, one supposes, suddenly appeared from the past. Aaron sought Moses' help to heal her and he interceded with God. All this appears to vindicate Moses in respect of his marriage to the Nubian woman.

---

1   R.K. Harrison notes that, as the verb in Numbers 12:1 is third person feminine singular, Miriam seems to be the spokesperson (*Numbers*, Wycliffe Exegetical Commentary, page 199).

The account of Josephus

Yet the puzzle remains: who was she? To answer this we have to consider a secular source. The Jewish historian Josephus[2] recounts how Moses was educated by the Egyptians. After a war with the Ethiopians, in which the Egyptians were totally overcome by their enemy, Moses was made general in charge of the army in the hope that their fortunes would be reversed. Moses did overcome the Ethiopians and drove them back into their own territory, where he besieged them at Saba, the royal Ethiopian city. The city was well nigh impregnable, located in a loop of the Nile with two tributaries making it virtually an island. The walls and ramparts of the city were massive and the natural 'moat' meant that the siege was likely to be protracted.

However, the Ethiopian king's daughter, Tharbis, watched Moses' military tactics and was greatly impressed. She fell in love with him and sent a servant with her offer of marriage to Moses. Moses, in return, accepted the offer on condition that the city surrendered to him. This was agreed and on taking the city, Moses married her and then he led the victorious Egyptian army back to their own land.

H. A. Whittaker is very scathing about Josephus' account: "There is no need to follow Josephus in his unbiblical fantasy about Moses leading a campaign against the Ethiopians, and falling in love with and marrying Tharbis, an Ethiopian princess." His own explanation is that Cush does not mean 'Ethiopia' but 'black'. He then links this to the black tents of Midian (Habakkuk 3:7)! Finally he writes, "This last clue is obviously the correct one here. Moses' Cushite wife was Zipporah, Jethro's daughter."[3] One can only wonder why, if this is so, the text does not name her and why Miriam and Aaron were so angry? Why should Zipporah not try to rejoin her husband?

---

2   See the section on this in Josephus, *The Antiquities of the Jews*, Book II, Chapter 10.

3   Whittaker, H. A. (1987) *Israel in the Wilderness*, page 105.

Some details of Josephus' full account stretch credulity but the general story is possible and seems probable: without it we have no explanation for this puzzling passage. It is also strange that Josephus should concoct such an elaborate story, unless it was part of Jewish folk-memory. Stephen's comment in Acts chapter 7 appears to give some support to the account in Josephus:

"And Moses was instructed in all the wisdom of the Egyptians; and he was mighty in his words and works."   (verse 22)

Refusing higher office in Egypt

We may also consider that the passage in Hebrews 11 is supportive, when it explains that Moses declined to accept higher office in Egypt, presumably some time later:

"By faith Moses, when he was grown up, refused to be called the son of Pharaoh's daughter; choosing rather to be evil entreated with the people of God, than to enjoy the pleasures of sin for a season; accounting the reproach of Christ greater riches than the treasures of Egypt: for he looked unto the recompense of reward."   (Hebrews 11:24-26)

The wording of this passage is a little unusual, but one would assume that it is saying that Moses declined to be adopted as Pharaoh's grandson.

However, the royal succession in Egypt was unusual in that it was through the female line and a Pharaoh ascended the throne only as a consequence of his marriage to a princess. Crown Princes often married their sisters in order to strengthen their claim to the throne. This unusual wording may imply that Moses could have been a potential claimant to the throne of Egypt. His refusal to enjoy "the pleasures of sin" and the "treasures of Egypt" also support this conjecture.

SUMMARY

The identity of the Cushite wife of Moses is explained by the account provided by Josephus, who states that she was an Ethiopian princess. She married Moses at the conclusion of a successful campaign he waged against Ethiopia (Nubia), when he was in charge of the Egyptian army (cf. Acts 7:22). The Cushite wife would have been Moses' first wife. He married Zipporah when in exile in Midian.

Jephthah's vow
(Judges 11:30,31)

THE account of how Jephthah came to make his vow in Judges 11 is straightforward. The spirit of the Lord came upon him (verse 29) as he went to fight against the children of Ammon and he vowed that, if the Lord would deliver them into his hand, then whatsoever came to meet him from the doors of his house on his return home would be offered as a burnt offering. It is evident from the fact that "whatsoever" is masculine that Jephthah envisaged an animal sacrifice.

On his return he was met by his only daughter and he was deeply distressed, saying:

> "Alas, my daughter! thou hast brought me very low, and thou art one of them that trouble me: for I have opened my mouth unto the LORD, and I cannot go back."　　　(Judges 11:35)

The record says that his daughter was supportive of his vow, but asked for a delay of two months to be with her companions in order to "bewail her virginity upon the mountains". After this she returned to her father "who did with her according to his vow which he had vowed" (verse 39). The puzzle is: what were the consequences of Jephthah's vow?

Making a vow

Firstly we need to be clear as to the nature of a vow. It is a solemn promise to God to undertake certain obligations which we enter into quite voluntarily. An early example is that made by Jacob:

> "And Jacob vowed a vow, saying, If God will be with me, and will keep me in this way that I go, and will give me bread to eat, and

raiment to put on, so that I come again to my father's house in peace, then shall the LORD be my God, and this stone, which I have set up for a pillar, shall be God's house: and of all that thou shalt give me I will surely give the tenth unto thee."

(Genesis 28:20-22)

The main obligation which Jacob voluntarily accepted in this vow was to offer "the tenth" of all the things which God gave him. This may reflect a code of laws which existed before the Law of Moses.[1]

Hannah, distraught that she was barren, made a vow asking that God would grant her to bear a son, whom she would devote to His service and who would be a Nazirite:

"And she vowed a vow, and said, O LORD of hosts, if thou wilt indeed look on the affliction of thine handmaid, and remember me, and not forget thine handmaid, but wilt give unto thine handmaid a man child, then I will give him unto the LORD all the days of his life, and there shall no razor come upon his head."   (1 Samuel 1:11)

She subsequently fulfilled her vow and Samuel was "given" to the Lord:

"For this child I prayed; and the LORD hath given me my petition which I asked of him: therefore I also have granted him to the LORD; as long as he liveth he is granted to the LORD. And he worshipped the Lord there."   (1 Samuel 1:27,28)

Making a vow was a serious matter and was regulated by the Law. If the vow related to the offering of an animal, once dedicated it could not be changed:

"And if it be a beast, whereof men offer an oblation unto the LORD, all that any man giveth of such unto the LORD shall be holy. He shall not alter it, nor change it, a good for a bad, or a bad for a good: and if he shall at all change beast for beast, then both it and that for which it is changed shall be holy."

(Leviticus 27:9,10)

---

1   It is evident that Abraham had a code of law which God had given to him before the Mosaic code (Genesis 26:5).

One could not offer the firstlings of clean animals for these were already devoted to God:

> "Only the firstling among beasts, which is made a firstling to the LORD, no man shall sanctify it; whether it be ox or sheep, it is the LORD's."   (Leviticus 27:26)

The firstlings of unclean animals had to be ransomed by paying the value of the animal and adding a fifth part or it could be sold at valuation (verse 27). This may be relevant in deciding the balance of probabilities regarding what happened to Jephthah's daughter.

On the other hand, anything devoted to God could not be redeemed:

> "Notwithstanding, no devoted thing, that a man shall devote unto the LORD of all that he hath, whether of man or beast, or of the field of his possession, shall be sold or redeemed: every devoted thing is most holy unto the LORD. None devoted, which shall be devoted of men, shall be ransomed; he shall surely be put to death."   (Leviticus 27:28,29)

One might consider that this passage is definitive, but it may specifically relate to the spoils of conquest which were "devoted", a word which may also be translated "utterly destroyed" (see, for example, Numbers 21:2 and margin, and also Joshua 10:40 and margin).

The seriousness of the obligation of fulfilling a vow is stressed in Ecclesiastes:

> "When thou vowest a vow unto God, defer not to pay it; for he hath no pleasure in fools: pay that which thou vowest. Better is it that thou shouldest not vow, than that thou shouldest vow and not pay."   (Ecclesiastes 5:4,5)

Later in Israel's history, the Rabbis absolved those who made a vow in good faith but were prevented from fulfilling it through no fault of their own. A good example of this would be the more than forty Jews who had vowed not to eat or drink until they had killed the Apostle Paul (Acts 23:12,13), but were thwarted by Claudius Lysius who conveyed him safely to Caesarea (verses 23-25).

The responses of Jephthah and his daughter

The distraught response of Jephthah on his return home reflects his recognition of the solemnity of a vow. He admits that he "cannot go back" on his word. This is matched by the response of Jephthah's daughter to his vow:

> "And she said unto him, My father, thou hast opened thy mouth unto the LORD; do unto me according to that which hath proceeded out of thy mouth; forasmuch as the LORD hath taken vengeance for thee of thine enemies, even of the children of Ammon."   (Judges 11:36)

Once more, her attitude may be a relevant factor in trying to decide what happened. Was she willingly accepting death or was she aware that the outcome would be otherwise? Competent Hebrew scholars are divided as to whether the text supports the belief that Jephthah's daughter was sacrificed or not. Some suggest that the brief statement that Jephthah "did with her according to his vow which he had vowed" (verse 39) is ominous and must indicate that she was sacrificed. Others question why, if that is the case, there is such emphasis on the daughter's virginity (verses 37-39) and that she and her companions spent two months "bewailing her virginity". As we are neither specifically told that Jephthah's daughter was offered as a burnt offering, nor that she remained alive, we can only weigh the probabilities.

Would she be an acceptable sacrifice to the Lord? The evidence on this is quite clear: the Law of Moses forbids such sacrifices:

> "When the LORD thy God shall cut off the nations from before thee, whither thou goest in to possess them, and thou possessest them, and dwellest in their land; take heed to thyself that thou be not ensnared to follow them, after that they be destroyed from before thee; and that thou inquire not after their gods, saying, How do these nations serve their gods? even so will I do likewise. Thou shalt not do so unto the LORD thy God: for every abomination to the LORD, which he hateth, have they done unto their gods; for even their sons

and their daughters do they burn in the fire to their gods."

(Deuteronomy 12:29-31)

And again the record says:

"There shall not be found with thee any one that maketh his son or his daughter to pass through the fire."

(Deuteronomy 18:10)

Other relevant passages are Leviticus 18:21 and 20:2-5. Sadly, as idolatry grew in Israel, these abominations were practised. This was the sin of Ahaz, who did not follow the example of David:

"But he walked in the way of the kings of Israel, yea, and made his son to pass through the fire, according to the abominations of the heathen, whom the LORD cast out from before the children of Israel."   (2 Kings 16:3)

The same detestable ritual was followed by Manasseh (2 Chronicles 33:6), adopting the idolatrous practices of nations that the Lord determined should be annihilated by Israel.

We may also take into account the case of Abraham and Isaac. Abraham obeyed God in attempting to sacrifice Isaac as a burnt offering, but the angel of the Lord intervened when Abraham's faith became evident. It is clear that the Lord did not want a human burnt offering and we learn from Hebrews that Abraham's obedience was predicated on his belief that God would raise Isaac from the dead. The parallel is helpful for Jephthah was "a mighty man of valour" and is commended by Samuel (1 Samuel 12:11) and the writer of Hebrews (11:32). His vow was made to the Lord in good faith at a time when the "spirit of the LORD" came upon him. Nothing is said in condemnation, which supports the belief that he did not sacrifice his daughter.

Devoted to the service of God?

What then did happen? If human burnt sacrifice was forbidden, then a godly man such as Jephthah would not have treated his daughter in this way. Yet the action taken was such that the daughters of Israel went to "celebrate" (or "lament", RV margin) the consequences each year. The emphasis on the daughter's virginity has already been noted above. This may offer a clue as to what happened. Was she devoted to the service of God at the tabernacle in much the same way that Samuel was "given" to God's service? Jephthah's vow was in two parts: "it shall be the LORD's" is then expanded and explained by, "and I will offer it up for a burnt offering". Since the latter part would not be acceptable to God with regard to his daughter, the first part could be fulfilled by giving her, not to a husband as would normally be the case, but to the service of the Lord. Hence the emphasis on her virginity – she would remain unmarried.

We have two passages which note the existence of women who served at the door of the tent of meeting:

"And he [Bazaleel] made the laver of brass, and the base thereof of brass, of the mirrors of the serving women which served at the door of the tent of meeting."   (Exodus 38:8)

"Now Eli was very old; and he heard all that his sons did unto all Israel, and how that they lay with the women that did service at the door of the tent of meeting."   (1 Samuel 2:22)

One must assume that these women were unmarried or widows since if they were married they would have family responsibilities, and in the case of Eli's sons their husbands would have taken appropriate action.

If these suppositions are correct, we might expect that each year the young women would visit Jephthah's daughter for four days, and this became a custom in Israel (Judges 11:40) to commemorate her devotion in accepting her father's vow, made in order to secure Israel from one of their major enemies.

H. A. Whittaker[2] notes the interesting suggestion that later, when the boy Samuel was returned to God by Hannah, he was entrusted to the care of Jephthah's daughter.

One important lesson comes from this episode for all generations:

"Be not rash with thy mouth, and let not thine heart be hasty to utter any thing before God; for God is in heaven, and thou upon earth: therefore let thy words be few." (Ecclesiastes 5:2)

---

2   Whittaker, H. A. (1989) *Studies in the Books of Judges and Ruth*, page 116.

SUMMARY

Vows must be fulfilled but there are no grounds for believing that Jephthah sacrificed his daughter. It is significant that the form of the vow is such that the offering of a male animal was assumed. Human sacrifice is abominable to God and there is no statement that she was killed. She remained unmarried; devoted to God for the rest of her life and almost certainly served along with other women at the tabernacle.

"Whose son art thou, thou young man?"

(1 Samuel 17:58)

AFTER David had slain Goliath we have two occasions when Saul made enquiries regarding the identity of this young hero. In 1 Samuel 17:55 Saul asks Abner, "Whose son is this youth?" and on learning that his identity is unknown, orders enquiries to be made. Then in verse 58 of the same chapter Saul asks David directly:

"Whose son art thou, thou young man? And David answered, I am the son of thy servant Jesse the Beth-lehemite".

That Saul should ask after the identity of David after the slaying of Goliath seems very strange, given that he had earlier sent a request to Jesse that David should come to him in order to ease his depression by playing the harp (1 Samuel 16:14-23). We are specifically told:

"And David came to Saul, and stood before him: and he loved him greatly; and he became his armourbearer. And Saul sent to Jesse, saying, Let David, I pray thee, stand before me; for he hath found favour in my sight."   (1 Samuel 16:21,22)

Later, when the stalemate developed in the war with the Philistines and the two armies faced each other in the valley of Elah, Goliath went out each day to taunt Israel with the proposition that the battle be settled by a single combat between a representative of Israel and himself. Given the fact that, when Saul was crowned, he stood head and shoulders taller than anyone in Israel (10:23) it would be reasonable to assume that he was probably the nearest match, physically, to Goliath. However, Saul was clearly unwilling to take up the challenge.

David encounters Saul once more

While David visited the battlefield in order to deliver food for his
brethren and a present of cheese to the captain of their thousand,
Goliath uttered his challenge once more. This defiance caused
dismay, both for Saul and the men of Israel. David offered to take
on the Philistine champion and, although initially rebuffed, he
persisted until this was accepted by Saul. The excuse for declining
his offer, initially, was spoken by Saul to David and included
the great difference in experience: David was but a youth and
Goliath had been a man of war from his youth. This conversation
is difficult to reconcile with Saul's question at the end of the
chapter.

In order to improve the apparently overwhelming odds
Saul wanted David to put on the royal armour. This indicates that
the "stripling" (17:56) was by this time as well-built as Saul and
contradicts the oft-depicted small boy fighting the giant. Having
first tried on the armour, helmet of bronze and a coat of mail,
David declined the offer, not because these were too big for him,
but because he had "not proved them" (verse 39). This contrasts
with his reliance on God's help, which he had proved and which
never failed. Once more we have a close dialogue between Saul
and David.

David saved the day by means of his sling and smooth
stone, felling and decapitating Goliath. The Philistines fled in
panic and were overcome by the pursuing Israelite army. After
all this, it seems that Saul is still unaware of the identity of the
young man whose faith changed the course of the war. How can
this be explained?

Textual difficulties?

Some Bible problems are alleviated to a greater or lesser extent
by a more accurate translation or, in some cases, by discovering
that the problem passage is absent from the best original texts.
In the case of this section of 1 Samuel, some of the difficulties
may be addressed by comparing the Hebrew text with that of
the Greek Septuagint (LXX). While this section of the Septuagint

often gives additional information over the Hebrew (Masoretic) text, in this part of 1 Samuel the sections 17:12-31 and 17:55-18:5 are absent. If this represents the original text then the problem is solved, for the two occasions when Saul enquires after David's identity (verses 55,58) are not in the Septuagint record. However, in recent years the earlier tendency of critics to accept the Septuagint over the Hebrew text, where these differ, has declined and unless there are overwhelming reasons for doing so priority is now almost always given to the Hebrew text. This is not, therefore, a satisfactory solution.

Out of sequence?

An alternative explanation is that the events recorded are not in chronological sequence. Again, in the past, critics had a field day cutting and pasting the texts in order to obtain a sequence which they felt to be more acceptable but recently this also has declined, perhaps because there was no consistency in the revisions that resulted.

There are some evident departures from a strict chronological sequence in chapter 17. For example, we are told in verses 54 and 55:

"And David took the head of the Philistine, and brought it to Jerusalem; but he put his armour in his tent. And when Saul saw David go forth against the Philistine, he said unto Abner, the captain of the host, Abner, whose son is this youth? And Abner said, As thy soul liveth, O king, I cannot tell."

(1 Samuel 17:54,55)

Here the events in verse 55 must have occurred before David had approached Goliath and the action described in verse 54, *after* the decapitation involved a journey to Jerusalem to place the head there, possibly on a spike outside the walls perhaps as if to say, in effect, 'you Jebusites will be next'. This accords with David's ambition, perhaps even from his youth, that Jerusalem should be the capital of the kingdom:

"LORD, remember for David ... How he sware ... and vowed ... Surely I will not come into ... my house ... Until I find out a place for the LORD, a tabernacle for the Mighty One of Jacob. Lo, we heard of it in Ephrathah ... For the LORD hath chosen Zion; he hath desired it for his habitation." (Psalm 132:1-13) The actual timing of this event would probably have occurred considerably later.

The record says David "put his armour in his tent", but this could not be David's tent, he was only a 'day-visitor' to the battle field, nor could it be David's armour for he had none, declining even to borrow Saul's armour. The armour was Goliath's and the tent the Lord's tabernacle as is evident from the account in 1 Samuel 21 of David's journey to Nob, where the tabernacle was located, seeking sustenance for his men and also a weapon:

"And David said unto Ahimelech, And is there not here under thine hand spear or sword? for I have neither brought my sword nor my weapons with me, because the king's business required haste. And the priest said, The sword of Goliath the Philistine, whom thou slewest in the vale of Elah, behold, it is here wrapped in a cloth ..."   (1 Samuel 21:8,9)

Returning to chapter 17, in verse 57 we are told:

"And as David returned from the slaughter of the Philistine, Abner took him, and brought him before Saul with the head of the Philistine in his hand."   (17:57)

It is evident that David brought the head to Saul soon after his triumph and then took it to Jerusalem later, as a means of psychological warfare, implying that the Jebusites would eventually suffer the same fate as the Philistines. Later they also were defeated by David (2 Samuel 5:6-9).

David's action may be compared with that of the Philistines when later they defeated Saul:

"And they put his armour in the house of the Ashtaroth: and they fastened his body to the wall of Bethshan."

         (1 Samuel 31:10)

Once again, this is not a satisfactory explanation since, apart from the small displacements considered above, the overall continuity of the record is evident.

A possible solution

It may be that the incidents described in 1 Samuel 16:15-23 include an element of anticipation of future events. Perhaps verses 15-17 are provided in order to explain how David, a young shepherd from an otherwise insignificant rural family, came to the royal court. Saul's immediate advisors suggested that his mental condition might respond to music and that a first-rate harpist should be sought. One of them happened to know of such a musician and that this young man was exceptional in other ways also. The king might not have assimilated the name of the young man, or his family. Many of us know the frustration of forgetting names almost as soon as we have heard them! The identity of the harpist would have little significance for Saul, especially if he was seriously disturbed at this time. The text implies this when it tells us that "an evil spirit from the LORD troubled" or "terrified" (margin) or "tormented" (NIV) him (16:14).

If David only entered the king's presence during his periods of illness, it may be that Saul was hardly aware of him and, on recovering, summarily dismissed him. It seems that David's involvement was intermittent:

"And it came to pass, when the evil spirit from God was upon Saul, that David took the harp, and played with his hand: so Saul was refreshed, and was well, and the evil spirit departed from him."   (1 Samuel 16:23)

"Now David went to and fro from Saul to feed his father's sheep at Bethlehem."   (17:15)

When, perhaps years later, David arrived at the battlefield and defeated Goliath he would have changed considerably and may not have been recognised by Saul. Even if he was known, it is important to notice that Saul does not ask, "Who is this?" but "Whose son is this youth?" (17:55). Abner was probably not present when David was engaged as court harpist and so he replied that he did not know. Saul then gave orders for him to find out: "Inquire thou whose son the stripling is" (verse 56). When the victorious David is presented to the king, carrying the grisly trophy, the question is the same: "Whose son art thou, thou young man?" (verse 58).

Why would the king be so interested in David's family? The answer seems to be hinted at in verse 26 where David asks what reward awaits the man who kills Goliath, and the answer in verse 27 is a repetition of what was disclosed in verse 25:

> "And the men of Israel said, Have ye seen this man that is come up? surely to defy Israel is he come up: and it shall be, that the man who killeth him, the king will enrich him with great riches, and will give him his daughter, and make his father's house free in Israel."   (1 Samuel 17:25)

David now qualified for financial rewards for himself and freedom from taxation for his family. Most significant, he would marry into the royal family by taking Merab, Saul's eldest daughter. Consequently, Saul would be concerned to know more of David's family, the members of which would thereby enjoy royal favours and close association with the royal family. We may conclude that Saul's questions were not asked to identify David but rather to establish his pedigree.

"The LORD was with him"

Saul did not honour his promise in this regard. There is no record of David receiving any financial reward, nor of exemption from taxation or royal service for his family. Merab was given to another man, Adriel the Meholathite (18:19) and Michal, Saul's second daughter, was earned with a grisly doubled bride-price (see 1 Samuel 18:25) intended by Saul to result in David's death at the hand of the Philistines.

However, David was not only "skilful in playing, and a mighty man of valour, and a man of war, and prudent in speech, and a comely person" (1 Samuel 16:18, ASV) but, most important of all, "the LORD was with him".

SUMMARY

The inability of Saul to recognise David when he went to fight Goliath is puzzling, especially when David had attended court to play the harp for him. It could be that when Saul was depressed and needed the musical therapy, he was not cognisant of the identity of his harpist and therefore did not recognise him later. It is also important to note that the key questions were not who David was but whose son he was. This would be significant if the reward for killing Goliath was indeed marrying into the royal household.

Saul and the witch of Endor
(1 Samuel 28:7)

S AUL sought the help of the witch of Endor because "when Saul inquired of the LORD, the LORD answered him not, neither by dreams, nor by Urim, nor by prophets" (1 Samuel 28:6). The puzzle in this case is why it appears that God did answer him by raising the prophet Samuel from the grave in order to intimate Saul's fate, given that God had forbidden consulting those with "familiar spirits"? Several times this is forbidden under the Law of Moses:

> "Turn ye not unto them that have familiar spirits, nor unto the wizards; seek them not out, to be defiled by them: I am the LORD your God." (Leviticus 19:31)

> "And the soul that turneth unto them that have familiar spirits, and unto the wizards … I will even set my face against that soul, and will cut him off from among his people." (20:6)

> "There shall not be found with thee … one that useth divination, one that practiseth augury, or an enchanter, or a sorcerer, or a charmer, or a consulter with a familiar spirit, or a wizard, or a necromancer. For whosoever doeth these things is an abomination unto the LORD." (Deuteronomy 18:10-12)

It is particularly ironic that Saul, who frequently disobeyed God's will, had actually followed the Law in this matter:

> "Now Samuel was dead, and all Israel had lamented him, and buried him in Ramah, even in his own city. And Saul had put away those that had familiar spirits, and the wizards, out of the land." (1 Samuel 28:3)

In desperation, Saul decided to consult his staff to locate a woman with a familiar spirit and was informed that there was one in Endor who had survived Saul's purge because, although it was assigned to the tribe of Manasseh, the town was never conquered:

"And Manasseh had in Issachar and in Asher Beth-shean and its towns, and Ibleam and its towns, and the inhabitants of Dor and its towns, and the inhabitants of En-dor and its towns ... Yet the children of Manasseh could not drive out the inhabitants of those cities; but the Canaanites would dwell in that land. And it came to pass, when the children of Israel were waxed strong, that they put the Canaanites to taskwork, and did not utterly drive them out." (Joshua 17:11-13, ASV)

Saul disguised himself by wearing clothes that would not suggest he was a king, and, accompanied by two servants, came to Endor by night, no doubt also to avoid detection. There, Saul asked her to use her occult arts to bring up someone whom he would name but she protested that he was setting a trap in order to execute her, stressing that Saul had done this previously to those with familiar spirits. It seems quite probable that, in spite of his attempted disguise, a man who was head and shoulders taller than most and had two servants, possibly arriving on asses, had been identified by the woman as King Saul. Further confirmation would arise when Saul assured her on oath that no punishment would follow. Who but the king could guarantee that?

When Saul named Samuel as the one that he wished her to bring up, the identity would be certain, for she would know that Samuel had been Saul's counsellor and she might also have heard that Saul could gain no answer from God by whatever means he had tried.

The séance now began and, pretending to see Samuel, the woman cried out loudly, no doubt for theatrical effect, and complained that Saul had deceived her but now she knew who he was. Thus identified, Saul would now have increased faith in her powers, and in his excitement sought to reassure her that no harm would come to her. Asking whom she had seen she did not say it was Samuel but that she saw "a god" coming up out of the ground. The Hebrew word she used was 'elohim, which is elsewhere used of judges, and Samuel was the last of the judges.

Now Saul asked for a description of what she saw and she replied that she could see an old man wearing a robe. While this was a rather vague description, the mention of the robe might suggest that this was indicative of a judge. Saul now jumped to the conclusion that the woman had brought up Samuel largely, one would imagine, because he was desperate to believe it, although the evidence was meagre and it seems that Saul saw nothing.

The next section is the most difficult to understand, for it appears as though Samuel, though dead, was actually speaking yet, as indicated above, it seems improbable that God would use this means of communicating with Saul when He had declined to do so through dreams, the Urim and Thummim and the prophets.

One possible explanation is hinted at in Isaiah 8:

"And when they shall say unto you, Seek unto them that have familiar spirits and unto the wizards, that chirp and that mutter: should not a people seek unto their God? on behalf of the living should they seek unto the dead?"   (Isaiah 8:19)

Not only is this a further condemnation of the practice of the occult but also a description of the methods used. The ESV describes the practitioners as "mediums and necromancers" and the NIV "mediums and spiritists" who "whisper and mutter". Even more helpful is a passage in Isaiah 29 which almost seems to be a description of the Endor séance:

"And thou shalt be brought down, and shalt speak out of the ground, and thy speech shall be low out of the dust; and thy voice shall be as of one that hath a familiar spirit, out of the ground, and thy speech shall whisper out of the dust." (29:4)

It is, therefore, almost certain that the woman practised ventriloquism, projecting her voice so that it seemed to come from the ground, and also simulated the voice of an old man, possibly in a quiet, croaking voice that one might expect an old man to have. The words can easily be understood as those which this perceptive woman would use, knowing who her 'client' was and his concerns. Note how she is able to make Saul give her the information she needs to maintain the deception, for she makes Samuel ask why he has been disturbed.

Saul replies, explaining his sore distress because the Philistines are warring against him, and God has abandoned him and no longer answers, not even through the prophets, nor by dreams. Samuel is his last hope and he asks that he may be guided as hitherto.

Armed with these details the woman would quickly be able to continue the charade. It was obvious that if God had abandoned Saul and was not willing to communicate with him, Samuel would be unable to indicate God's intentions. So she uses this as a means of avoiding any detailed information. The Philistines are not the only enemy, God is now his adversary. Knowing the historical background of reasons for Saul's rejection through his disobedience, and the anointing of David as the king-in-waiting, she relates this as though Samuel was explaining that his fate was now sealed. God has abandoned him; he has made David his enemy and the Philistines are sure to win the impending battle, adding that he and his sons would perish. Under the circumstances, this prediction had a high probability. The words were:

> "Moreover the LORD will deliver Israel also with thee into the hand of the Philistines: and tomorrow shalt thou and thy sons be with me: the LORD shall deliver the host of Israel also into the hand of the Philistines."   (1 Samuel 28:19)

Of course, if she proved wrong about the last prediction, Saul would be unlikely to punish her. How could he defend such action if he had actually gone to this woman, knowing her to be a woman with a familiar spirit, and sought her help? He would be guilty of hypocrisy.

Hearing what he feared, Saul collapsed full length upon the ground, partly because of the news but also because in his hasty journey, he had eaten nothing that day or during the night. The woman offered him refreshment but at first he declined it.

Further encouragement by the woman and his servants, who no doubt were hungry, caused him to relent and a meal consisting of the fatted calf and unleavened bread was served. This would have a benefit for the woman because, although Saul had promised that she would come to no harm, she was evidently still anxious (verse 21). A shared meal in ancient cultures indicated fellowship and, consequently, peace. This explanation, based on the comments in Isaiah 8 and 29, adequately accounts for what happened and does not depend on ideas that are contrary to other scriptures.

Ancient oracles were consulted in much the same way as people today read their horoscopes. In some cultures important decisions, particularly in matters of business, are not taken without first consulting the omens. The skill with which these predictions are made and personal horoscopes compiled, relying on only providing generalities which therefore have a high probability, is impressive. More remarkable is the willingness of clients to believe them, even when they have provided details which the astrologer or clairvoyant can use to their advantage. However, a moment's thought will show that, as there are only twelve signs of the zodiac, one in twelve (a little over eight per cent) of the population should have exactly the same experiences each day!

SUMMARY

The problems in the account of the witch of Endor are why God seems to have raised Samuel from the dead and participation in a procedure which He expressly forbids. The woman would easily recognise that a man much taller than average with servants was the king in disguise. The psychological insight of those who claim to be able to contact the dead would enable her to assess what Saul wanted. Careful analysis of the text suggests that Saul did not actually see Samuel, for he asks what the woman could see. She almost certainly used ventriloquism (cf. Isaiah 29:4) and played on the desperation of Saul to obtain some response from the God who had now abandoned him. Her prediction was relatively obvious given the state of affairs in Israel.

The death of Saul
(1 Samuel 31; 2 Samuel 1)

THE suicidal death of King Saul is recorded for us in 1 Samuel 31:4, but in 2 Samuel 1:10 we have the apparently contradictory account of the Amalekite's 'mercy killing' of the mortally wounded Saul. How can these two versions be reconciled?

It should be noted that in the Hebrew Bible the two books of Samuel form a single book and therefore these accounts occur in consecutive chapters of the same volume. The writer would be quite aware of an apparent contradiction and so we may conclude that there is, as always, a rational explanation for the apparent differences in the inspired account.

The death of Saul
The account in 1 Samuel 31 describes how Saul was hit by archers and was "sore wounded" (verse 3, KJV). Saul would be incapacitated and, fearing that the Philistines would abuse or mock him as he was dying, he commanded his armour-bearer to despatch him with his sword. The armour-bearer was understandably reluctant to do this, so Saul fell on his own sword and died (verse 4). On witnessing this, the armour-bearer did likewise and died alongside his sovereign (verse 5).

On the following day, when the Philistines came to strip the bodies of the dead, they discovered Saul and his three sons. The record continues:

"And they cut off his head, and stripped off his armour, and sent into the land of the Philistines round about, to carry the tidings unto the house of their idols, and to the people. And they put his armour in the house of the Ashtaroth: and they fastened his body to the wall of Bethshan."

(1 Samuel 31:9,10)

Note that the record says nothing of Saul's crown or his bracelet, which are mentioned in the Amalekite's account in 2 Samuel 1:10. This gives some credence to the Amalekite's account but, when we examine what he said to David, there are some anomalies.

The Amalekite messenger

Turning to the record in 2 Samuel we learn that, following the defeat of the Amalekites who had raided Ziklag, David's base, carrying off the women and children and great spoil (1 Samuel 30:1,2), David had remained in Ziklag for two days. On the third day a stranger arrived at the city. He was dishevelled and had earth on his head. On enquiring where he had come from, the man explained that he had escaped from Israel's camp and, on further enquiry, that Israel had been defeated by the Philistines. Furthermore, Saul and Jonathan were dead.

Perhaps because he was reluctant to believe the news, David asked the young man how he knew this. The man replied that he happened by chance to be on Mount Gilboa and had seen Saul in his chariot, leaning on his spear, while the Philistine chariots were in pursuit behind him.

This raises the question of why he "happened by chance" to be there. Twice in the account we are told that the stranger was an Amalekite (2 Samuel 1:8,13). Since David had recently pursued the Amalekite raiders of Ziklag we might suppose that he was associated with this group. However, Gilboa, the site of Saul's death is located about 110 miles (168 km) north-east of Ziklag. Add to this the fact that Amalekite territory was to the south-east of Ziklag, it is difficult to understand why this young man 'just happened' to be so far north. One wonders whether he had anticipated the defeat of Israel by the Philistines and had gone north to see whether he could gain wealth by stripping the dead. It is evident from what follows that he was seeking material benefit by bringing news and tokens of Saul's death to David.

The young man then recounted how Saul had turned in his chariot and called to him and had asked who he was. On answering that he was an Amalekite, Saul had asked him to put him out of his misery by slaying him. It would seem that Saul was anxious not to be captured by the Philistines and subjected to mockery or abuse, but would willingly die at the hands of a man from another of Israel's enemies, the Amalekites! The young man then explained that, forming the opinion that Saul was indeed mortally wounded, he acquiesced, stood on him and despatched him.

A possible reconciliation?

This account has similarities with that given in 1 Samuel 31, but the evident differences raise questions as to whether this young man was telling the truth. Attempts have been made to reconcile the two accounts. For example, Josephus[1] says that when his armour-bearer refused to kill him, Saul attempted to fall on his sword but, in spite of several attempts to force the sword through his body, it appears that he was too weak to do this. On turning and seeing the Amalekite, Saul asked him to put him out of his misery by forcing the sword through him, and he complied. Saul's armour-bearer then took his own life. Such a reconstruction is possible but not consistent with the Amalekite's account. The most satisfactory explanation of the puzzle is that the Amalekite was not telling the truth, or at least not the whole truth.

It may be that the Amalekite witnessed some part of what is recorded in 1 Samuel 31 and decided to turn this to his own advantage by claiming that he had disposed of Saul, whom he believed to be David's enemy, and thereby expect a reward. After all, Saul's armour-bearer had killed himself and there would probably be no other living witnesses. Even if he had merely stumbled across the bodies of Saul and his armour-bearer, and

---

1   Flavius Josephus, *Complete Works* (trans. W. Whiston), "Antiquities of the Jews", Book 6, Chapter 14, paragraph 7 (page 146 in Kregel Edition, 1963).

invented a possible scenario, who would be able to contradict it? Why not take the credit for the demise of Saul and turn the situation to his own advantage?

The young man then produced Saul's crown and his bracelet in support of his claim. This was incontrovertible evidence: Saul must be dead and it was highly probable that Jonathan was also dead. It is interesting that he said he had brought the tokens "unto my lord". Although he did not specifically ask for a reward, this phrasing suggests that he expected one.

At this point David tore his clothes as a sign of grief and his men followed suit, mourning for Saul and Jonathan. The rest of the day was spent in weeping and fasting, not only for Saul and his sons, but also for "the people of the LORD, and for the house of Israel". This was a black day: after many years of warfare, the Philistines had finally killed the king of Israel.

David's interrogation

David now enquired who this man was. He explained that he was the son of a stranger, that is, an alien and an Amalekite. There is a sad irony about this situation. Earlier Saul had been commanded by Samuel to destroy the Amalekites:

> "Thus saith the LORD of hosts, I have marked that which Amalek did to Israel, how he set himself against him in the way, when he came up out of Egypt. Now go and smite Amalek, and utterly destroy all that they have, and spare them not; but slay both man and woman, infant and suckling, ox and sheep, camel and ass."   (1 Samuel 15:2,3)

Saul and the people failed to obey this divine directive and now an Amalekite was the bearer of the news of Saul's death in battle against the Philistines and was carrying his crown.

David asked how it was that he did not fear to raise his hand against the Lord's anointed? As the son of an alien resident in Israel he would be familiar with some aspects of Israel's culture and may have heard how David had refused to raise his hand against Saul when, on several occasions, the opportunity presented itself. Certainly David regarded him as guilty and declared:

> "Thy blood be upon thy head; for thy mouth hath testified against thee, saying, I have slain the LORD's anointed."
>
> (2 Samuel 1:16)

The reward that the Amalekite received for claiming to have killed Saul in order to gain material benefit for himself was the loss of his own life.

We may conclude that while it may be possible to reconcile the accounts in general, as Josephus suggested, the differences in the details indicate that the most satisfactory explanation is that the Amalekite was not entirely truthful, being motivated by the prospect of a reward from David.

SUMMARY

The differing accounts of the circumstances of Saul's death, which in 1 Samuel 31 is suicide but in 2 Samuel 1 is a 'mercy killing' by the Amalekite, can be reconciled if Saul's suicide attempt failed and the Amalekite despatched Saul at his request. However, the difference in the detail is probably a consequence of the Amalekite's attempt to gain a reward from David.

11

"And Satan came also among them ..."
(Job 1:6)

THE discourses between the Lord and Satan recorded in the first two chapters of the Book of Job must present problems for those who believe in a personal devil, since it is difficult to reconcile the possibility that God, who is of "purer eyes than to behold evil" and who cannot "look on iniquity" (Habakkuk 1:13) would discuss the merits of Job with the one whom they regard as the source of all evil. This dialogue is, however, not without its problems even for those who understand the true nature of the Hebrew word *satan* and the Greek διαβολος, *diabolos*. How are we to reconcile our concept of the justice and righteousness of God with Job's dreadful suffering – inflicted, it seems, in order to correct the misapprehensions of his satan? Here was a unique man, "perfect and upright, and one that feared God, and eschewed evil". Job was one of the three men, along with Noah and Daniel, whom God said "should deliver but their own souls by their righteousness" (Ezekiel 14:14) in the event of divine judgements being inflicted on the land. Yet it appears that he was subjected to dreadful suffering simply in order to prove that God's estimate of him was correct and the adversary's was mistaken. Does this seem ethical?

Job's adversary
If, as some believe, the assembly of "the sons of God" took place in the 'court of heaven', then it is an angel who is Job's adversary and who discusses Job's character with the Almighty, inferring that Job's upright behaviour is superficial and, in reality, only

'cupboard love'. It is evident, as the Lord Jesus has explained that, unlike God, the angels are limited in their knowledge (Matthew 24:36). Even so, one would imagine that an angel would gladly accept the assurances of the Almighty and not question His judgement on the matter. This, and the issue of doubtful ethics, suggests that an alternative scenario is required in order to reconcile the apparent contradictory evidence.

An alternative view is to regard the assembly of the sons of God as a meeting of the faithful. Job's adversary would then be a member of the worshipping congregation whose assessment of Job was that he appeared to be genuinely dedicated to God's service but in reality it was only his wealth and influence that enabled him to do this and, were he to lose them, the real Job would be evident. Not only did his wealth and power shield him from the problems that other worshippers experienced but his dedication was motivated by self-interest. Job only served God because he believed that this would ensure continued prosperity. Stripped of his riches and authority, Job would be just like everyone else.

Perhaps Job's adversary had said as much to other members of the congregation. If not, God knew of these thoughts and intended to demonstrate their speciousness and vindicate Job. However, we are still left with a problem that Job lost his wealth and family in order to make evident his loyalty to God. We also have to resolve the ethical problem of the death of all his children as part of that attestation.

When it became evident that Job did not blame God or lose his faith, the adversary suggested that, should Job's health deteriorate, his true character would be revealed. Once more God acquiesced, yet Job's dreadful sufferings only demonstrated his spiritual fortitude. The problem of the ethics now becomes even more intense. How are we to reconcile the justice of God and the infliction of suffering on His "servant" Job, unique amongst those on earth, a "perfect and upright" man who "feared God and eschewed evil"? The divine accolade could hardly be greater.

Job's children

The answer appears as the story unfolds. There was a grain of truth in the adversary's assessment of Job. It appears in the opening of the book, where Job offered sacrifices vicariously for his sons and daughters, in case they had sinned and renounced God in their hearts (1:5). This is virtually an insurance policy, yet Job should have known that such an offering would not be acceptable since if his children had offended it was necessary that they admit their sin when the offering was made. It is significant that all we are told about his children is that day after day they 'ate, drank and were merry' and, when they were "eating and drinking wine in their eldest brother's house", the building collapsed around them in a storm and they were killed: 'tomorrow they died'.

Indeed, we may perhaps suspect that Job knew his children were not godly, that they were sinners and had renounced God. If this is correct then their demise was not simply part of the lesson for the adversary but divinely appointed just retribution. This ethical problem is therefore resolved.

A purpose in suffering

Later we learn from Job's own lips that his godly behaviour was motivated, at least in part, by anxiety that his wealth and health might be taken away:

> "For the thing which I greatly feared is come upon me, and that which I was afraid of is come unto me. I was not in safety, neither had I rest, neither was I quiet; yet trouble came."
>
> (Job 3:25,26, KJV)

These anxieties are common to us all. Perhaps Job thought that his piety and philanthropy (29:12-17) would ensure his continued wealth and health. Yet in his heart he knew that there would be no guarantees, as he admitted later. The wicked, who have no inclination to serve God, prosper (21:7-15) and those who are devoted to God's service are not exempt from suffering. The truth of this is nowhere more evident than in the life of the Son of God who "though he were a Son, yet learned he obedience by the things which he suffered" (Hebrews 5:8, KJV). If this was a necessary experience for the sinless Son of God, who can claim exemption?

Eventually Job confessed that although God was apparently unwilling to explain the reasons for his suffering, there could be a purpose in it:

"But he knoweth the way that I take; when he hath tried me, I shall come forth as gold."   (Job 23:10)

Eliphaz had earlier hinted that there might be a purpose in Job's calamities when he said:

"Behold, happy is the man whom God correcteth: therefore despise not thou the chastening of the Almighty."   (5:17)

This comment is repeated in Proverbs 3:11, cited by the writer of Hebrews (12:5,6) and confirmed by the Lord Jesus (Revelation 3:19).

Of course, Job did finally come forth as gold, for "the LORD blessed the latter end of Job more than his beginning" (Job 42:12). Job also learned a vital lesson from his experiences. Although he had questioned God's treatment of him, when asked what he knew of God's creative work and how the universe was sustained (chapters 38 and 39), he confessed: "I know that thou canst do all things, and that no purpose of thine can be restrained" (Job 42:1,2). The ethical problem is again solved: Job also needed to learn obedience by the things that he suffered. He came through the valley of the shadow of death still trusting in God and emerged the better for it. His previous anxieties were now diminished, his faith strengthened.

His experiences were "written aforetime ... for our learning, that through patience and through comfort of the scriptures we might have hope" (Romans 15:4). We are privileged 'to see behind the scenes' as it were, and understand that the origins of Job's sufferings were not the result of divine ill-will towards him, but in order "that the man of God may be perfect". His endurance in adversity is recorded to encourage us all:

"Behold, we count them happy which endure. Ye have heard of the patience of Job, and have seen the end of the

Lord; that the Lord is very pitiful, and of tender mercy."

(James 5:11, KJV)

May that be our experience when the One whom Job prefigured returns: God's servant who was indeed unmatched in all the earth, perfect and upright and who feared God and eschewed evil, who was made perfect through dreadful sufferings and was heard in that he feared, and being made perfect, he became the author of eternal salvation unto all them that obey him (Hebrews 5:7-9).

SUMMARY

In scripture, a 'satan' is simply an adversary for good or for evil. If the opening of Job is set in the 'court of heaven' we have an ethical problem: that a godly man is to suffer loss of health, wealth and family in order to convince an angel that his assessment of Job is mistaken. If, however, it is the assembly of believers, where aspersions are cast on the authenticity of Job's faith by one member of the congregation, then this would make sense. In reality, remarkably faithful though he was, Job is not without fault. There is a sense in which he does show a degree of 'cupboard love'. He confesses that he had concerns he might lose his wealth and influence, admitting that what he feared has actually happened and he could not prevent it. Ultimately he comes through his troubles a better man.

"Answer not a fool … Answer a fool according to his folly"
(Proverbs 26:4,5)

P ERHAPS it is significant that the Hebrew language has at least five words for "fool". Divine wisdom, it seems, recognizes several different kinds of fool. Although they differ in Hebrew, the words for "fool" are descriptive of kinds of people whose characteristics overlap. In other words, these 'fools' have a great deal in common! Young's Concordance[1] gives them as 'Fool', 'Boaster', 'Self-confident', 'Empty-person' (*nabal*) and 'Thick-headed'.

The word for fool in this proverb is the third in the list above, $k^e sil$, meaning dense, stupid, self-confident. This kind of fool is one who accepts general opinions without question. Today we might say that he is the product of a poor education, influenced more by celebrity culture and tabloid newspapers.[2] He prefers his comfortable illusions to the stark reality. Such a person considers his own opinions to be the only ones that matter and displays his ignorance readily.

We read in Proverbs:

"Like a lame man's legs that hang limp is a proverb in the mouth of a fool … Like a thornbush in a drunkard's hand is a proverb in the mouth of a fool."   (26:7,9, NIV)

---

1   Young, R. (1939) *Analytical Concordance to the Holy Bible*, Lutterworth press, page 360.
2   Popular tabloid newspapers were so-called because their format was smaller than the more serious ones and their English was much simpler. Complex issues were often reduced to easily assimilated views that supported the political inclinations of their proprietors.

Worst of all, this fool is a menace and wastes your time. Once he gets an idea in his head nothing will stop him. So, keep out of his way if you can:

"Better to meet a bear robbed of her cubs than a fool in his folly."   (Proverbs 17:12, NIV)

The full quotation of this puzzling passage is:

"Answer not a fool according to his folly, lest thou also be like unto him. Answer a fool according to his folly, lest he be wise in his own conceit."   (Proverbs 26:4,5)

The RV margin indicates that "in his own conceit" is literally in the Hebrew "in his own eyes" and is so rendered in the NIV:

"Do not answer a fool according to his folly, or you will be like him yourself. Answer a fool according to his folly, or he will be wise in his own eyes."

At first sight it seems that these two consecutive verses of scripture contradict one another, for in verse 4 we are advised *not* to answer a fool according to his folly and in verse 5 we *are* recommended to answer him according to his folly! This has given Bible critics ammunition to say that the Bible contradicts itself and, superficially, it is evident why these critics claim that there is a contradiction. What is strange is that they did not ask themselves why the compiler of the Proverbs, a book about wisdom, had not noticed this apparent contradiction!

Surely the whole point of the juxtaposition of these two verses is to teach us that fools have to be dealt with in different ways, depending on the situation and the second part of each statement expresses the two contrasting ways of dealing with fools. One way of coping is to avoid responding to them; another approach is not to suffer them gladly and the choice depends on the actual situation.

The former approach (verse 4) applies when someone is being foolish and one's first inclination is to consider what they say or do and respond in similar vein. Yet it may be wiser simply to ignore them, just as you might do when insulted. In this way, simply refusing to answer them becomes a silent but severe rebuke. In effect, ignoring their comment implies two things: it is not worth the effort of responding and even if one did, they would be unable to understand. Proverbs counsels such a response:

> "A fool shows his annoyance at once, but a prudent man overlooks an insult."   (Proverbs 12:16, NIV)

Put another way, a foolish comment needs no answer; it would be casting "pearls before swine".

The tactic in chapter 26:5 is to be used when the fool is obviously incapable of understanding a sensible answer. To try to deal with him at a rational level will just be a waste of effort. However, simply to ignore him would suggest, in his mind, that you are unable to answer and he was correct in what he said or did. Therefore, in this case, in order to prevent his 'getting away with it', you are reduced to giving a 'foolish' answer but one which he can understand at his level. The very fact that you are meeting him on his own terms, and at his level, should demonstrate to him that he has not got the better of you and it might make him think more deeply as you respond in a 'foolish' way.

Paul seems to have used this tactic in 2 Corinthians 11 where he says:

> "I repeat: Let no-one take me for a fool. But if you do, then receive me just as you would a fool, so that I may do a little boasting."   (2 Corinthians 11:16, NIV)

His reason is given later in verse 19: "You gladly put up with fools since you are so wise!" (NIV) and again in verse 21: "I am speaking as a fool." If they listen to fools then if Paul 'admits' he is a fool, perhaps they will now listen to him. In the next chapter he continues this tactic:

> "I have made a fool of myself, but you drove me to it. I ought to have been commended by you, for I am not in the least inferior to the 'super-apostles', even though I am nothing."
>   (2 Corinthians 12:11, NIV)

The sarcasm of his comment regarding the ones whom the Corinthians regarded as the "super-apostles" is certainly answering fools according to their folly!

SUMMARY

While this proverb appears to be contradictory, there are occasions when it is better to ignore the fool's folly lest the impression is given that his comments are worth recognising, and others where it is necessary to provide a suitable counter-argument lest the fool assumes that the point is valid and cannot be gainsaid.

New Testament

13 |

"If therefore thine eye be single ..."
(Matthew 6:22,23; Luke 11:34)

T HIS saying of the Lord Jesus is virtually the same in Matthew 6 and Luke 11 but Matthew includes an additional comment:

"The light of the body is the eye: if therefore thine eye be single, thy whole body shall be full of light. But if thine eye be evil, thy whole body shall be full of darkness. If therefore the light that is in thee be darkness, how great is that darkness!"
(Matthew 6:22,23)[1]

"The light of the body is the eye: therefore when thine eye is single, thy whole body also is full of light; but when thine eye is evil, thy body also is full of darkness." (Luke 11:34)

The statement that the "light" of the body is the eye, where "light" is the Greek, λυχνος, *luchnos*, an oil lamp, suggests that the eye is not a window but the source of illumination for the body. This is in accord with the final statement regarding the darkness which results from the opposite state. It is, therefore, strange that a "single" eye or lamp should appear to be preferable to two eyes or two lamps. We also note in both these passages that "single" is contrasted with "evil", which are not normal opposites. This suggests that the rendering "single" may be misleading.

An idiom

The Greek word 'απλους, *haplous* (and its derivative 'απλωτες, *haplotes*) does normally mean 'single' or 'simple', but it seems

---

1   Quotations in this chapter are from the KJV unless otherwise indicated.

that in this case it may be an idiomatic usage. This is where a concordance can be of help, for we find that it is translated variously in other contexts. For example, in Romans 12:8 Paul exhorts, "he that giveth, let him do it with simplicity (RV, *liberality*; RV margin, Greek, *singleness*)". Here the word clearly means 'generously'. Again, in 2 Corinthians 8:2, Paul extols the generosity of the Macedonian ecclesias, noting "that in a great trial of affliction the abundance of their joy and their deep poverty abounded unto the riches of their *liberality*" (Greek, *haplotes*). Later in the same letter he thanks God, "being enriched in every thing to all *bountifulness*" (Greek, *haplotes*) and comments two verses later about the Corinthians' "*liberal* distribution"[2] to the poor in Jerusalem (9:11,13).

Another aspect of this word is seen in Paul's exhortations to servants (slaves) in the kind of service which they should give to their masters. In Ephesians 6:5 they are to serve "with fear and trembling, in singleness (*haplotes*) of your heart, as unto Christ", that is, with a generous spirit. The same exhortation is given to slaves in Colossae: they are to perform their duties "not with eyeservice, as menpleasers; but in singleness (*haplotes*) of heart, fearing God (Colossians 3:22). In James 1:5 the adverb (*haplos*) is used of God "that giveth to all men *liberally*, and upbraideth not".

An evil eye

It appears, then, from its New Testament usage that "single" often means 'generous'. This also accords with the Jewish idiom, in which 'a good eye' is a metaphor for liberality and an 'evil eye' for niggardliness. The Law of Moses warned Israel against meanness in the year of release:

> "Beware that there be not a thought in thy wicked heart, saying, The seventh year, the year of release, is at hand; and thine eye be evil against thy poor brother, and thou givest him nought; and he cry unto the LORD against thee, and it be sin unto thee."   (Deuteronomy 15:9)

---

2   The Greek is literally "liberality (*haplotes*) of the fellowship (*koinonia*)", or "sharing" or "participation".

The effect of prolonged siege, when food would be so scarce, is described in the following passage:

"The man that is tender among you, and very delicate, his eye shall be evil toward his brother, and toward the wife of his bosom, and toward the remnant of his children which he hath remaining ... The tender and delicate woman among you, which would not adventure to set the sole of her foot upon the ground for delicateness and tenderness, her eye shall be evil toward the husband of her bosom, and toward her son, and toward her daughter." (Deuteronomy 28:54,56)

Similar ideas are to be found in the book of Proverbs:

"Eat thou not the bread of him that hath an evil eye, neither desire thou his dainty meats." (Proverbs 23:6)

"He that hasteth to be rich hath an evil eye, and considereth not that poverty shall come upon him." (28:22)

One Proverb is quite revealing:

"He that hath a bountiful eye shall be blessed; for he giveth of his bread to the poor." (22:9)

The phrase "he that hath a bountiful eye (RV margin, Hebrew, good)" is translated in the Septuagint (the Greek Old Testament) as "he that pities the poor".

One passage confirms the idea that an "evil" eye is a mean disposition. In the Parable of the Vineyard, when the workers who have worked all day complain that they have received the same pay as those who have worked only one hour, the householder asks:

"Is it not lawful for me to do what I will with mine own? Is thine eye evil, because I am good?" (Matthew 20:15)

This "evil eye" was the exact opposite of the householder's generous spirit. It would also be the opposite of a "single" or bountiful spirit.

Barclay[3] translates and also interprets these key words, for in Matthew 6 he renders "single" as "sound and generous"

---

3   Barclay, W. (1968) *The New Testament, A New Translation, Vol. 1*, Collins, London, pages 68 and 325.

and "evil" as "diseased and grudging". It is also significant that the context of this passage in Matthew (but not Luke) is one in which the Lord Jesus is warning against materialism and serving mammon.

A generous spirit

The lesson from this puzzling passage now becomes clear. If we have a generous spirit our whole way of life is enlightened, but if we harbour a mean and grudging outlook then we are walking in darkness. If our efforts are directed to accumulating earthly riches we shall fail to set our hearts on heavenly treasure. There is a saying of the Lord Jesus, not to be found in the Gospel records, which encapsulates this. Paul informs us:

> "I have shewed you all things, how that so labouring ye ought to support the weak, and to remember the words of the Lord Jesus, how he said, It is more blessed to give than to receive."
>
> (Acts 20:35)

The single, that is, generous eye, will fill us with the light of Christ.

SUMMARY

The word "single" might suggest single-mindedness but it is associated in other contexts with generosity where is it contrasted with an evil or grudging disposition. The Lord's teaching infers that a generous attitude is spiritually enlightening for he said, "It is more blessed to give than to receive".

"The kingdom of heaven suffereth violence …"

(Matthew 11:12)

T HERE is general agreement amongst commentators that this is indeed a most enigmatic passage. The wide variety of disparate explanations offered provides striking evidence of this. The similar, but simpler, comment in Luke 16 does not really help to clarify the situation:

"The law and the prophets were until John: since that time the kingdom of God is preached, and every man presseth into it."

(Luke 16:16)[1]

In Luke the meaning is clearer than in Matthew, yet the verb "presseth" is the same as "suffereth violence" in Matthew 11 (Greek βιαζομαι, *biazomai*). Part of the problem in Matthew arises from the Greek text itself, where two interpretations are possible. If the verb in the first part is in the middle voice then it means 'come forcibly', but if it is passive then it means 'suffer violence'. Similarly, the following phrase can mean 'forceful people seize it' or 'violent persons plunder it'.

Bruce[2] notes that the NEB rendering of Luke 16:16, "Everyone forces his way in", suggests "something like a universal gate-crashing" which is at odds with the teaching of the Lord Jesus elsewhere in which the limited access is stressed (Matthew 7:13,14; Luke 13:24). He offers the proposition that Luke's meaning is that we have to show determined effort in order to gain entry.

---

1 Quotations in this chapter are from the KJV unless otherwise indicated.
2 Bruce, F. F. (1983) *The Hard Sayings of Jesus*, pages 113-118.

Hostility towards the kingdom

The context of this puzzling passage is a reference to the work of John the Baptist:

> "And from the days of John the Baptist until now the kingdom of heaven suffereth violence, and the violent take it by force. For all the prophets and the law prophesied until John."
>
> (Matthew 11:12,13)

John was the last of a long line of prophets of whom many, if not most, suffered violence. It would not be unreasonable to say that "the kingdom of heaven" had always "suffered violence". It is fascinating to note how often the Lord Jesus was to draw attention to this sad state of affairs:

> "Blessed are ye, when men shall revile you, and persecute you, and shall say all manner of evil against you falsely, for my sake. Rejoice, and be exceeding glad: for great is your reward in heaven: for so persecuted they the prophets which were before you."   (Matthew 5:11,12)

Again:

> "... If we had been in the days of our fathers, we would not have been partakers with them in the blood of the prophets. Wherefore ye be witnesses unto yourselves, that ye are the children of them which killed the prophets. Fill ye up then the measure of your fathers ... O Jerusalem, Jerusalem, thou that killest the prophets, and stonest them which are sent unto thee ..."   (Matthew 23:30-32,37)

and again:

> "Therefore also said the wisdom of God, I will send them prophets and apostles, and some of them they shall slay and persecute: that the blood of all the prophets, which was shed from the foundation of the world, may be required of this generation."   (Luke 11:49,50)

In the end, the Lord too must suffer at the hands of God's chosen race:

> "Nevertheless I must walk today, and tomorrow, and the day following: for it cannot be that a prophet perish out of Jerusalem."   (Luke 13:33)

Something similar was predicted for the Lord's disciples (Matthew 10:17-22,28,38,39). John the Baptist was arrested and ultimately beheaded. The Lord himself was betrayed, handed over to the occupying Roman power and executed. For generations, Israel had eagerly anticipated the coming of Messiah's reign, yet instead of a welcome for the kingdom there was hostility. Truly, the kingdom of heaven was suffering violence when it should have been received with joy and gratitude.

"The violent take it by force"

What are we to make of the comment that "the violent take it by force"? Certainly, attempts were made to do just that in the case of the Lord Jesus. John records that, following the feeding of the five thousand:

> "When Jesus therefore perceived that they would come and take him by force, to make him a king, he departed again into a mountain himself alone."   (John 6:15)

The attitude of the crowds during the triumphal entry into Jerusalem was indicative of the popular sentiment with regard to a king "like the nations round about", who would free them from the oppressive yoke of Rome. Within days, their fickle loyalty had evaporated and they confessed that they "had no king but Caesar"! A further clue to the Lord's remarks may be found in his comments to Pilate:

> "Jesus answered, My kingdom is not of this world: if my kingdom were of this world, then would my servants fight, that I should not be delivered to the Jews: but now is my kingdom not from hence."   (John 18:36)

The temptation in the wilderness, that the Lord should use the power of the Spirit to claim all the kingdoms of the world, was rejected even though there was apparent scriptural support (Psalm 2:8). One day the Father's promise, that he should be given the heathen for his inheritance, and the uttermost parts of the earth for his possession, would be fulfilled, but not by human warfare. Those who "took the sword would perish with the sword" (Matthew 26:52) as the events leading up to the

Roman annihilation of the Jewish revolt in AD 70 so poignantly illustrated. So the cross must precede the crown: the glory would certainly follow, but in the day which the Father appointed.

SUMMARY

The accounts in Matthew and Luke may seem similar but it may be that in Luke the emphasis is on intense personal effort to gain entry into the kingdom while in Matthew the reference is to the suffering by the prophets, of whom John the Baptist was the last. The attempts to make the Lord Jesus a king by force are also relevant.

"What is bound on earth will be bound in heaven"
(Matthew 16:19; 18:18)

I T must be significant that this assurance by the Lord Jesus is recorded twice in Matthew's Gospel. At first sight, there appears to be little in these verses that is hard to comprehend. It seems that the Lord is rewarding the Apostle Peter by granting him absolute authority as a consequence of his confession in response to the question of the Lord's identity. Earlier (verses 13,14) the Lord had asked whom men were saying that he was, and this prompted several possibilities: John the Baptist, Elijah, Jeremiah or one of the other prophets. Then he asked for the view of the disciples and this elicited the response from Peter: "Thou art the Christ, the Son of the living God" (verse 16). The Lord then commented that Peter had been blessed by the Father in revealing this to him, for it was not the depth of knowledge that one would expect from "flesh and blood", that is, human reasoning. The earlier variety of the views held by the general populace showed how inadequate this was.

Now the Lord used a play on Peter's Gentile name to emphasise the significance of his response:

"And I also say unto thee, that thou art Peter, and upon this rock I will build my church; and the gates of Hades shall not prevail against it." (Matthew 16:18)

Peter is the Greek Πετρος, *Petros*, which means a stone or pebble but the word "rock" is πετρα, *petra*. This negates the idea that Peter was the first 'pope' and that the church (εκκλησια, *ecclesia*) would be founded on him. The Lord would not select a loose stone but a solid rock of faith as the basis of his church.

What follows has been mistranslated in order, it would seem, to compound the false doctrine of the church being founded on Peter as the first 'pope'. In most versions it reads as in the KJV / RV:

"I will give unto thee the keys of the kingdom of heaven: and whatsoever thou shalt bind on earth shall be bound in heaven; and whatsoever thou shalt loose on earth shall be loosed in heaven." (Matthew 16:19)

Later, in chapter 18, following a consideration of the treatment of a disciple whose behaviour has been unacceptable, the ultimate sanction is exclusion from the fellowship of the community. As if to confirm the authority conveyed in chapter 16, now apparently extended beyond Peter, as the 'thou' becomes 'ye', the Lord says:

"Verily I say unto you, what things soever ye shall bind on earth shall be bound in heaven; and what things soever ye shall loose on earth shall be loosed in heaven." (Matthew 18:18)

The combination of the apparent founding of the church on Peter and the assurance that whatever he, and now the collective authority of the church, decides to bind or loose on earth will be bound or loosed in heaven, has formed the basis of absolute ecclesiastical authority, especially of Roman Catholicism and Protestantism.

It does not, therefore, come as a surprise to discover that this is a false translation of the original Greek. J. B. Phillips has noted that the Greek construction is not what Peter "binds on earth" will be "bound in heaven", but rather "what *has been bound* in heaven" he will bind on earth. He goes on to comment: "There is a world of difference between guaranteeing celestial endorsement of the Apostle's actions and promising that his actions guided by the Holy Spirit will be in accordance with the Heavenly pattern".[1]

---

1   Phillips, J. B., in the Foreword to Marshall, A. D. (1959) *The Interlinear Greek-English New Testament*, page iii.

This construction does not, however, occur in most English translations. It is found, of course, in the interlinear text of the Marshall Greek-English Interlinear New Testament, the NET Bible and The Kingdom of God Version, and also as an alternative in the margin of the ESV.

SUMMARY

The Greek of this phrase indicates that the initiative is not with Peter, who would oblige heaven to endorse his decision, but that what Peter decides will already have been decided in heaven and communicated to him by the Holy Spirit.

Moses and Elijah in the Transfiguration
(Matthew 17:3; Mark 9:4; Luke 9:30)

TWO problems are raised by this incident: was it merely 'a vision' as Matthew 17:9 suggests, or were Moses and Elijah actually present? The former is quite possible since it was one means by which prophets received their message, for example Abraham (John 8:56), Balaam (Numbers 24:4) and Habakkuk (3:7). The latter is more problematical for it would involve the premature, if temporary, resurrection of these prophets.

Some assistance is afforded by the Lord's pronouncement at the end of Matthew 16 and the parallels in Mark and Luke. These are set out for comparison below (quoting from the ASV):

Matthew 16:28	Mark 9:1	Luke 9:27
"Verily I say unto you, there are some of them that stand here, who shall in no wise taste of death, till they see the Son of man coming in his kingdom."	"And he said unto them, Verily I say unto you, There are some here of them that stand by, who shall in no wise taste of death, till they see the kingdom of God come with power."	"But I tell you of a truth, There are some of them that stand here, who shall in no wise taste of death, till they see the kingdom of God."

Although the wording is not quite identical, the information is the same, namely:

- The information to be imparted is significant.
- It applies only to some of those who were close by and could hear it.

- These individuals would not die before it happened.
- They would see the Lord Jesus coming with power in God's kingdom.

The Lord selected Peter, James and John and they went up into a high mountain. The time interval mentioned in all three accounts may be a clue as to the location of the mountain. Superficially, it appears that the selection of the three disciples occurred after a week or so, but the text in Matthew and Mark says the Lord "bringeth" them up into a high mountain, not 'taketh'. In other words, this is written from the perspective of the destination, not the starting point. This technique is used elsewhere in scripture, for example when Noah was commanded to "come ... into the ark" (Genesis 7:1). If this is correct, the journey to the mountain and the ascent took about a week.

We now need to ascertain the starting point of the journey. The last mentioned location is "the parts / villages of Caesarea Philippi" (Matthew 16:13; Mark 8:27) which is located at the most northerly part of the Tetrarchy of Philip, almost on the border with the Roman province of Syria and about twenty-five miles (forty km) north of the northern shore of Lake Galilee. The nearest possible "high mountain" is in the Mount Hermon range, some thirty miles (fifty km) to the north-east. While the distance on a map is relatively short, the height of 9,230 feet (2,814 m) would take some time to ascend. The fact that the disciples were "heavy with sleep" (Luke 9:32) may be indicative of a gruelling climb after a walk of some days. It is snow-capped all the year round and this may have significance, as will be considered below.

While the Lord "was praying, the fashion of his countenance was altered, and his raiment became white and dazzling" (Luke 9:29). Matthew and Mark say he was "transfigured", the Latin equivalent of the Greek μεταμορφooμαι, *metamorphomai*, literally 'transformed', to change shape or form. Paul uses the same word in Romans 12:2 when he exhorts us, "Be not fashioned according to this world: but be ye *transformed* by the renewing of your mind". Matthew explains what the change was, in words similar to Luke: "His face did shine as the sun, and his garments became white as the light", while Mark says, "His garments became glistering, exceeding white so as no fuller on earth can whiten them". If this occurred in the snowfield, the effect would have been enhanced by the reflection of this light.

At this point, "two men" (Luke) appeared, identified as Moses and Elijah (also in Matthew; Mark has Elijah and Moses) and began talking with the Lord. They "appeared in glory" which seems to imply that this is post-resurrectional glory and may have a significant bearing on our understanding of the transfiguration. We may add to this the Lord's earlier comments regarding those who would see "the Son of Man coming in his kingdom" and "the kingdom of God come with power" before their deaths. This implies that they would experience the reality of this future kingdom.

One can understand that Elijah might be readily identified if he wore the characteristic garments of a "raiment of camel's hair and a leathern girdle about his loins" but Moses' identity might have been less obvious unless he had the shining face (Exodus 34:30) which "sent forth beams" (RV margin) which, unfortunately, in Hebrew is literally 'horns' and was so depicted by many classical artists. It is possible, of course, that the Lord greeted them by name.

The nature of the conversation is given only by Luke:
"And behold, there talked with him two men, who were Moses and Elijah; who appeared in glory, and spake of his decease which he was about to accomplish at Jerusalem."
(Luke 9:30,31)
The topic was the forthcoming decease (Greek *exodos*, exit) which he was about to accomplish in Jerusalem. This presents us with a problem of timing for if Moses and Elijah are, effectively, resurrected in glory then they are in the future kingdom but they are speaking of an event "which he was about to accomplish", that is, still to occur.

If, as noted earlier, this was only a vision and not a reality, it is difficult to see what benefit it would have for the Lord Jesus with respect to the discussion that Moses and Elijah had about

the Lord's decease. He knew that this was his destiny and he
knew the details:

> "Behold, we are going up to Jerusalem, and the Son of Man
> will be betrayed to the chief priests and to the scribes and be
> delivered into the hands of sinful men and will be mocked and
> insulted and they will spit on him; and they will condemn him
> to death and deliver him to the power and the authority of
> the governor and to the Gentiles to be crucified; and they will
> scourge him, and kill him."[1]

On the other hand, if this was a real experience of the future,
then its impact would be the greater. The concept of 'time travel'
may seem to be more appropriate for science-fiction literature
but the everlasting God is not constrained by time. Indeed, as
the Apostle Paul declares in Romans 4, He "calleth the things
that are not, as though they were" (verse 17), and the prophets
invariably used the past tense in their divine predictions because
the outcome was so certain.

If this was a real experience and the future had, as it were,
travelled back to the present,[2] this would be of great comfort to
the Lord, for the words of Moses and Elijah would indicate that
his commission would end in success. His rejection and suffering
would not be lessened but it would not be in vain.

Here we meet the paradox of predestination and free
will. The purpose of God could never be thwarted and yet it has
always been achieved within the context of human free will from
Eden until now. If the Lord Jesus could not have failed then it
is evident that the outcome could not be regarded as a success.
His prayer in Gethsemane implies that failure was possible.
The prospect of his foreknown extreme suffering was not the
worst factor; rather that the whole purpose of God rested on
his shoulders. The fulfilment of the promises to Abraham and to

---

1 Composite citation from Matthew 20:19; 26:2; Mark 10:33,34; Luke 18:32,33;
   20:20; 24:7.
2 There would be no difficulty for the Eternal God, who is from everlasting to
   everlasting and not a prisoner of time as we are, in arranging 'time travel' in which
   the present was transported into the future or the future brought back to the
   present.

David depended on him. His triumph was not a 'hollow victory' and for this reason "God highly exalted him, and gave unto him the name which is above every name …" (Philippians 2:9).

Earlier Peter, James and John were heavy with sleep but awakened at the arrival of Moses and Elijah (Luke 9:32). It may be that this was a symbolic death and resurrection as in the case of Daniel (8:18; 10:9,10) and John (Revelation 1:17) which, if so, fits the futuristic context. Once awake, they witnessed the Lord's glory and the encounter with Moses and Elijah.

The time came for Moses and Elijah to depart. Peter did not want the experience to end and uttered the understatement of all time: "Lord it is good for us to be here." His suggestion that he should construct three booths, one each for the Lord, Moses and Elijah, was made in desperation, "for he wist not what to answer" (Mark), "not knowing what he said" (Luke). Fear now came upon the privileged three as a bright cloud overshadowed them. From this cloud they heard the divine voice: "This is my beloved Son, my chosen, in whom I am well pleased, hear ye him." At this, they fell on their faces as the fear continued. The Lord now touched them, saying that they should arise and not be fearful. On looking round they saw only the Lord Jesus. As they descended from the mountain the Lord insisted that they should not disclose what they had witnessed until after his resurrection from the dead.

Peter never forgot this experience and recounted it later in his second letter:

"For we did not follow cunningly devised fables, when we made known unto you the power and coming of our Lord Jesus Christ, but we were eyewitnesses of his majesty. For he received from God the Father honour and glory, when there was borne such a voice to him by the Majestic Glory, This is my beloved Son, in whom I am well pleased: and this voice we ourselves heard borne out of heaven, when we were with him in the holy mount."   (2 Peter 1:16-18, ASV)

It may be that John also was referring to this when he wrote:

"And the Word became flesh, and dwelt among us (and we beheld his glory, glory as of the only begotten from the Father), full of grace and truth." (John 1:14)

The Letter of James contains no allusion to the transfiguration and this is possibly a further indication that the author was James the Lord's brother. James the son of Zebedee was executed quite early by Herod Agrippa I and probably did not have the opportunity to write about his experience in the mount.

SUMMARY

It seems most likely that what the disciples observed in the Mount of Transfiguration was not a vision but the actual presence of Moses and Elijah as a consequence of 'time travel' to the kingdom, since their discourse with the Lord concerned a yet future event with respect to the disciples time frame while the actual discussion of it seems to be retrospective. If this suggestion should be considered improbable, it should be remembered that God is not constrained by time and "with God all things are possible".

"Elias is come already ..."
(Matthew 17:12; Mark 9:13)

THIS enigmatic comment of the Lord Jesus, recorded by both Matthew and Mark, was made in response to a question posed by the disciples as they descended from the Mount of Transfiguration. They had just witnessed the presence of Elijah and Moses talking with the Lord, but were puzzled regarding his comment about their having to keep confidential what they had witnessed until the Son of Man had been raised from the dead. Although they discussed what it might mean amongst themselves (Mark 9:10), they were also concerned as to why it was that the scribes said that Elijah must come first.

One may imagine that the scribes had an ulterior motive in stressing this and were implying that the Lord must be an impostor when he proclaimed that the kingdom was at hand, for Malachi had declared that Elijah would come first (4:5).

"In the spirit and power of Elias"
Some had thought that John the Baptist was indeed Elijah. He dressed like Elijah with a girdle of leather about his loins (2 Kings 1:8) and spoke uncompromisingly, just as Elijah had done. Before John's birth, Zacharias had been told by the angel:

> "He shall go before him in the spirit and power of Elias, to turn the hearts of the fathers to the children, and the disobedient to the wisdom of the just; to make ready a people prepared for the Lord." (Luke 1:17)[1]

---

1 Quotations in this chapter are from the KJV unless otherwise indicated.

The very phrase, "turn the hearts of the fathers to the children" was an unmistakeable citation of Malachi 4:6. No wonder then, that some were persuaded that John the Baptist could indeed be Elijah. However, John knew that he was not in reality Elijah for, when this suggestion was put to him, he emphatically denied it (John 1:21).

At first sight we seem to have a contradiction. John the Baptist was quite categorical that he was not Elijah, while the Lord affirms that "Elias is indeed come, and they have done unto him whatsoever they listed, as it is written of him" (Mark 9:13). Furthermore, in Matthew's account, in response to the disciples' question, "Why then say the scribes that Elijah must first come?" the Lord explained:

> "Elijah indeed cometh, and shall restore all things: but I say unto you, that Elijah is come already, and they knew him not, but did unto him whatsoever they would. Even so shall the Son of man also suffer of them. Then understood the disciples that he spake unto them of John the Baptist."
>
> (Matthew 17:11-13, ASV)

Verse 12 is the clue which helps explain the apparent incongruity of the Lord's affirmation and John's denial. The next verse completes the resolution of the dilemma:

> "And if ye will receive it,[2] this is Elias, which was for to come ..."   (Matthew 11:14)

It is also in harmony with the comment made earlier in Matthew 11 where the Lord affirms that John fulfilled the terms of Malachi 3:1:

> "For this is he, of whom it is written, Behold, I send my messenger before thy face, which shall prepare thy way before thee."   (Matthew 11:10)

This provides the key to the apparent contradiction. If they had been willing to receive John, then the nation would have responded and been ready to accept the Lord Jesus as their Messiah. He was not a resurrected Elijah but, as the angel

---

2   Or *him*, RV margin.

had intimated to Zacharias, he would "go before … in the spirit and power of Elijah". Sadly, the nation was not willing and in the rejection of John the Lord saw his own rejection to come: "Likewise shall also the Son of man suffer of them" (17:12).

In this episode we have the familiar paradox of free will and predestination at work simultaneously. Israel was given the opportunity to accept Christ as King and rejected him. Divine foreknowledge "provided some better thing for us, that they without us should not be made perfect".

SUMMARY

The apparent contradiction between John the Baptist's insistence that he was not Elijah and the Lord's affirmation that Elijah had already come is resolved by the Lord's explanation that, had Israel been willing to accept the one who came "in the spirit and power of Elijah" as his forerunner, then his own kingdom could have been inaugurated. Sadly, they did not accept John as the "Elias that was for to come" and consequently they rejected the Lord also.

"If thy brother sin against thee ..."

(Matthew 18:15)

T HE Lord Jesus said:
"And if thy brother sin against thee, go, shew him his fault between thee and him alone: if he hear thee, thou hast gained thy brother. But if he hear thee not, take with thee one or two more, that at the mouth of two witnesses or three every word may be established. And if he refuse to hear them, tell it unto the church: and if he refuse to hear the church also, let him be unto thee as the Gentile and the publican." (Matthew 18:15-17)

The puzzle here is that this verse seems at odds with the Lord's teaching. In the Lord's Prayer we are taught to ask for forgiveness for our trespasses, as we forgive those that trespass against us (Matthew 6:12; Luke 11:4) and the Lord continues by explaining:

"For if ye forgive men their trespasses, your heavenly Father will also forgive you. But if ye forgive not men their trespasses, neither will your Father forgive your trespasses." (Matthew 6:14,15)

Later in chapter 18, Peter asks the Lord how frequently he must forgive his brother:

"Then came Peter and said to him, Lord, how oft shall my brother sin against me, and I forgive him? until seven times?" (18:21)

It might be thought that Peter had not been listening, but the Lord's response shows quite clearly that he had, for the answer was:

"I say not unto thee, Until seven times; but, Until seventy
times seven."   (18:22)

It would take considerable effort to count the number of
times until a total of 490 had been reached. The actual figure
is thought to be based on an increased reversal of the boast of
Lamech:

"If Cain shall be avenged sevenfold, truly Lamech seventy and
sevenfold."   (Genesis 4:24)

Yet the chapter appears to open with a description of the
three stages that should be followed in dealing with the brother
or sister who sins against you. The first stage is to indicate that
you 'have a bone to pick' and make the offending party aware
of your grievance. If this fails to secure an apology or remedy
then it will be necessary to ask one or two others to assist in
trying to gain satisfaction. It would be more likely to succeed if
it became evident that others supported your case. If this fails
then the whole ecclesia must be involved and failure to elicit a
satisfactory result means that the offending party is to be placed
out of fellowship. This procedure is about as far from the answer
given later to Peter's question as is possible. Peter was told that
he must forgive seventy times seven.

How are we to reconcile this apparent discrepancy? The
answer is that some manuscripts do not include "against thee".[1]

If, as seems likely in the context of the chapter, this was
not the original text, then this passage is dealing with an entirely
different problem. What is involved here is the action to be taken
when a brother or sister becomes aware of a significant departure
from the standard of behaviour expected on the part of another
brother or sister.

The procedure outlined above is now seen in a quite
different light, for it is evidently intended as a means of securing
repentance. The one who has learned of the sin must encounter
the sinner alone. If the offender is challenged and admits the sin

---

1   Metzger, B. M. (1994[2]) *A Textual Commentary on the Greek New Testament*, page 36,
     suggests that "against thee" is an early interpolation, perhaps having been copied
     from verse 21.

and ceases to continue to commit it, then, in the Lord's words, "if he hear thee, thou hast gained thy brother". The matter is closed: only two people know of it in addition to God and the Lord Jesus. If this first attempt fails, then the assistance of others must be sought in the hope that the seriousness can be brought home and the offender persuaded to repent. Should this fail to secure a change then there is no option but to make it an ecclesial matter which, if unsuccessful may lead to disfellowship.

The context of this teaching fully supports the view that it is not a procedure for gaining satisfaction in a dispute. It is also supported by the Lord's Prayer, in which we are to forgive those that trespass against us. The immediately preceding verses are concerned with the recovery of lost sheep:

> "For the Son of man came to save that which was lost. How think ye? if any man have a hundred sheep, and one of them be gone astray, doth he not leave the ninety and nine, and go unto the mountains, and seek that which goeth astray? And if so be that he find it, verily I say unto you, he rejoiceth over it more than over the ninety and nine which have not gone astray. Even so it is not the will of your Father who is in heaven, that one of these little ones should perish."
>
> (Matthew 18:11-14, ASV)

In the parallel account in Luke 15:3-7 the Lord adds to this parable the parables of the lost coin and the prodigal son, which further supports the view that the context is recovery of that which was lost and not obtaining personal satisfaction.

The disciple's obligation is to endeavour to recover an erring brother or sister when this becomes known to them. Only later in Matthew 18 does Peter raise the question of what should be done in the case of a personal offence.

SUMMARY

The words "against thee" in the text of Matthew 18:15 are missing from some manuscripts and are thought to be an interpolation. If so, the subject of this passage is not about a procedure for securing personal satisfaction when we are offended but rather a means of recovering an erring brother or sister. The context and other scriptures support this conclusion. Only later in the chapter does Peter ask what should done in the case of personal offences.

Easier for a camel to go through the eye of a needle ...

(Matthew 19:24; Mark 10:25; Luke 18:25)

A T first sight, this saying of the Lord Jesus, if taken literally, is impossible. There is no way that a camel could pass through the eye of a needle. Even if we assume that it is hyperbole, that is, an exaggeration for effect, arresting the attention of the hearer in order to make a serious point, it still seems difficult to understand. It would mean that there is no possibility for a rich man to enter the kingdom. This conclusion was evident in the reaction of the disciples on hearing the saying: "Who then can be saved?" In a world where the rich virtually had everything, it might have come as a surprise to learn that they could not use their riches to buy their way into the kingdom. Presumably, it means that their riches are more likely to be a hindrance to entry into the kingdom, not an absolute barrier. One only has to consider men like Abraham or Job to see that it is not absolute disqualification.

At one time, the exposition of this passage was based on the belief that, in ancient cities, in addition to the normal city gates, a much smaller gate, called "the eye of a needle" was provided so that, when the large gates were closed at the end of the day in order to secure the safety of the city, this smaller gate could be readily defended, while open, and any late arrival of a loaded camel could be accommodated and allowed entry. Its load, however, would have to be removed in order to allow access. The analogy was then made that the only way a rich man could enter the kingdom was to rid himself of his wealth in much the same way that a loaded camel would have to be divested of its burden in order to pass through the 'eye of a needle' gate.

Some credence is given to this idea in the comment by the Lord Jesus regarding the width of the way and the dimensions of the gate that admits entry into the kingdom:

"Enter ye in by the narrow gate: for wide is the gate, and broad is the way, that leadeth to destruction, and many be they that enter in thereby. For narrow is the gate, and straitened the way, that leadeth unto life, and few are they that find it."

(Matthew 7:13,14)

This comment does not imply that entry is impossible but only that it is difficult. If the view that a rich man must divest himself of his wealth is correct, then one would have to suggest that Abraham (and the other patriarchs) and King David, given their wealth, would be at serious risk, even though one was "the friend of God" and the other "a man after God's heart".

The suggestion that cities had, in addition to the main gates, some smaller gates that were called "the eye of a needle" finds no evidence in reality. Rather it seems that this explanation was derived from the necessity of finding an explanation of the passage under consideration. A strong piece of supporting evidence is that Matthew and Mark use the ordinary word for a needle, ῥαφις, *rhaphis*, while the word used by Luke, in 18:25, refers to a surgical needle, that is, βελονη, *belonē*, a natural usage for a medical practitioner. This would imply that a needle is indeed the subject and not a small, auxiliary gate.

If this is the case then another explanation is needed. One possibility is that the Lord Jesus was using hyperbole in this case, as he often did[1] but not in such an extreme way as to contemplate attempting to try to have a camel pass through the eye of a needle. In fact, he may not have used the word 'camel' at all. The word for a camel in Greek is καμηλον, *kamēlon*, while the word for a rope or cable is καμιλον, *kamilon*, which would

---

1   For example: Matthew 5:29,30; 11:25; 23:24; Mark 10:21; Luke 9:23,24; 13:19; 17:6; John 6:53,54.

be pronounced similarly. Some manuscripts actually have this latter word. It may be that one or more scribes misheard the word while listening to a reader dictating the text as they wrote a further copy.

While we still have hyperbole, a figure of speech that we noted above was often used by the Lord Jesus, it seems more appropriate to say that it is easier for a rope to go through the eye of a needle, rather than imagine attempting to do this with a camel.

SUMMARY

The conventional explanation of this passage, that ancient cities had in addition to their normal gates a much smaller one, called "the eye of a needle", which could be used after the main gate had been closed, is not supported by historical evidence. This concept is essential to the conventional explanation for it supposes that a camel could be brought through the smaller gate, but only after its burden of goods (representing riches) had been unloaded. The Greek words for 'camel' and 'rope' are spelled differently, by a change of a vowel, but would be pronounced almost identically. If a scribe heard "camel" instead of "rope" then this would explain the difference. The saying still incorporates hyperbole, but it seems more plausible that the original saying was: "It is easier for a rope to go through the eye of a needle than for a rich man to enter the kingdom of God." Some manuscripts have this version of the Lord's saying.

The Lord's promise to the malefactor on the cross

(Luke 23:43)

T HE answer of the Lord Jesus to the request of the malefactor that the Lord would remember him when he came into his kingdom, as normally punctuated, was: "Verily I say unto thee, Today shalt thou be with me in Paradise." This implies that, before the day was ended, both the Lord and this man would be in Paradise. The puzzle is created by the clear and copious scripture teaching that the Lord was in the tomb until the third day,[1] at which time he arose and appeared first to Mary Magdalene, and the other women. Later that day (Luke 24:13) he appeared to the two disciples travelling to Emmaus and on their return to Jerusalem they discovered that the Lord had appeared to Simon. At that moment, he appeared to the eleven apostles. Even more problematic is the Lord's comment to Mary Magdalene after she lingered at the tomb:

"Touch me not; for I am not yet ascended unto the Father: but go unto my brethren, and say to them, I ascend unto my Father and your Father, and my God and your God."

(John 20:17)

These factors raise the question, where was the malefactor while the Lord was in the tomb and subsequently before he ascended to his Father? Another question is why the Lord chose to say that the malefactor would be with him in Paradise. The only two other uses of this word are in 2 Corinthians 12:4 and Revelation 2:7.

---

1 See Matthew 16:21; 17:23; 20:19; 27:64; Mark 9:31; 10:34; Luke 9:22; 13:32; 18:33; 24:7,21,46; 1 Corinthians 15:4.

In the former, Paul relates the experiences of someone, presumably himself, caught up into the third heaven, which he equates with Paradise, where he heard words that could not be expressed. Paul explains this in terms which suggest he himself hardly understood his Paradise experience. But if Paradise is equated with heaven, the Lord's promise is even more difficult to explain: as we have seen, he did not ascend the day he died, but on the third day afterwards.

In the Revelation passage we read:

"He that hath an ear, let him hear what the Spirit saith to the churches. To him that overcometh, to him will I give to eat of the tree of life, which is in the Paradise of God."

(Revelation 2:7)

This is in accord with the origin of the word Paradise, derived as it is from an ancient Persian word for a walled garden. In the Old Testament, the Hebrew derivative, *pardēs*, is used in Nehemiah 2:8 to denote the "kings' forest" and in Ecclesiastes 2:5 the writer says: "I made me gardens and parks (Hebrew, *pardēs*), and I planted trees in them of all kinds of fruit ..."

The original 'park' was, of course, the Garden of Eden:

"And the LORD God planted a garden eastward, in Eden; and there he put the man whom he had formed. And out of the ground made the LORD God to grow every tree that is pleasant to the sight, and good for food; the tree of life also in the midst of the garden ..."   (Genesis 2:8,9)

This links with the usage in Revelation 2:7, above, where the tree of life is mentioned. The Lord Jesus and the malefactor were being executed on a tree of death; a cross. It is called a tree in several New Testament passages. For example, when the apostles were arraigned before the Jewish Council they accused them of Christ's death:

"The God of our fathers raised up Jesus, whom ye slew, hanging him on a tree."   (Acts 5:30)

When Peter preached to Cornelius he used the same phrase:

"And we are witnesses of all things which he did both in the
country of the Jews, and in Jerusalem; whom also they slew,
hanging him on a tree." (10:39)

Paul, preaching about Christ in Antioch said:

"And when they had fulfilled all things that were written of
him, they took him down from the tree, and laid him in a
tomb. But God raised him from the dead." (13:29,30)

In Galatians, Paul explains the significance of crucifixion:

"Christ redeemed us from the curse of the law, having become
a curse for us; for it is written, Cursed is every one that
hangeth on a tree." (Galatians 3:13)

Peter, once more, in his first letter, says:

"For hereunto were ye called: because Christ also suffered for
you ... who his own self bare our sins in his body upon the
tree ..." (1 Peter 2:21,24)

The word "cross" (literally a 'stake') is also used, but it is
evident that the link with trees is significant for it became for
those who believe, in effect, a tree of life. This, surely, is the
reason the Lord Jesus used the word 'paradise'. One malefactor
railed on the Lord, but the other, in his few words from the cross,
indicated his acceptance of his rightful punishment and also his
knowledge of the Lord Jesus and his purpose:

"But the other answered, and rebuking him said, Dost thou
not even fear God, seeing thou art in the same condemnation?
And we indeed justly; for we receive the due reward of our
deeds: but this man hath done nothing amiss. And he said,
Jesus, remember me when thou comest in thy kingdom."
(Luke 23:40-42)

The malefactor's knowledge is remarkable: he knew that the Lord
Jesus was innocent of any crime; possibly that he was never
convicted of sin; certainly that he would rise again from death;
and that Jesus would return to establish a kingdom at some
future date for he actually said, "when thou shalt have come into
thy kingdom". He also showed faith in the possibility that he,
although being put to death for his deeds, could be raised by the
Lord when the Lord came again. It seems quite probable that

he was once a disciple but, seeing that the Lord was not willing to use force to establish Jewish sovereignty, had joined the freedom-fighters led by Barabbas and wielded the sword against the Romans. Now he could not move his arms as they were nailed to the wood. Perhaps, at last he recognised that the Lord's way was the right way.

We began by suggesting that the normal punctuation, which implies that the malefactor and the Lord would be in paradise that day, could not be correct. In fact, there are good additional reasons why it must be challenged. The original Gospel texts had no punctuation, and not even spaces between the words. More importantly, if a comma is to be inserted it must be after the word "Today" not before. It is a common Hebrew idiom to say "I tell you this day ..." or "today". An example is to be found in Deuteronomy 4, where Moses says:

> "I call heaven and earth to witness against you this day, that ye shall soon utterly perish from off the land whereunto ye go over the Jordan to possess it."   (Deuteronomy 4:26)

In this case the Lord stresses the solemnity of his statement by the addition of "truly" (*amen*) for further emphasis. All the factors considered above combine to suggest that what the Lord actually said was: "Verily I say unto thee today, thou shalt be with me in Paradise."

SUMMARY

The promise to the malefactor on the cross could not mean that he would be with the Lord in Paradise that day for the Lord was in a tomb until the third day. The Lord emphasises the certainty of his promise by the common phrasing of the time: "Truly I tell you today, that ..." The original Greek text was not punctuated.

"Out of his belly shall flow rivers of living water"
(John 7:37,38)

T HIS passage is one which has exercised the resourcefulness of scholars over a considerable period, not least because it has proved impossible to find an Old Testament scripture that fits the Lord Jesus' citation, "Out of his belly ..." etc. The phrase "living water" occurs frequently and its various uses may assist us in understanding this, otherwise enigmatic, passage of scripture.

The full quotation is:

"In the last day, that great day of the feast, Jesus stood and cried, saying, If any man thirst, let him come unto me, and drink. He that believeth on me, as the scripture hath said, out of his belly shall flow rivers of living water."

(John 7:37,38, KJV)

There are two puzzling aspects of this passage: to whom does this refer and where is the scripture that is said to be fulfilled? Taking the first aspect, it is possible to translate the original Greek in three ways and distinguished scholars are divided as to the correct rendering.[1] The version above clearly indicates that it is the one who believes on the Lord Jesus from whom the rivers of waters will flow. It is possible to arrange the lines of the text into a poetic format which also changes the meaning, as follows:

"... If anyone thirst, let him come [to me];
And let him drink who believes in me.

---

1 Brown, R. E. (1971) *The Gospel according to John*, The Anchor Bible, Vol. 1, pages 320,321.

As the scripture says,
'From within him shall flow rivers of living water'."[2]

This arrangement implies that it is from Christ that the rivers of water flow. In passing, the literal rendering of the Greek κοιλιας, *koilias*, as "belly" in the KJV, is given as "within" by some versions / translators, including Brown[3] and Bruce[4] who renders it as "inmost being". This anatomical location was regarded as the seat of the emotions in ancient cultures while we tend to use 'heart'. Their use of 'heart' is equivalent to our use of 'mind', that is the brain.

It is also possible to arrange the text so that it is ambiguous as to the identity of the one from whom the waters originate, but this avoids the question and takes us no further. The next verse, however, explains that the "rivers of water" is a reference to the Holy Spirit:

"But this spake he of the Spirit, which they that believed on him were to receive: for the Spirit was not yet given; because Jesus was not yet glorified."   (John 7:39)

The Lord Jesus or disciples?

We are now better able to decide whether this indicates that, as the alternative rendering above implies, the Lord Jesus is the source of the Holy Spirit. While it is true that the Holy Spirit gifts were conveyed from the apostles by the laying on of hands, the ultimate source was the Lord Jesus. Hence we may conclude that he is the source of the rivers of water. This accords with the solution to the remaining problem: where does scripture reveal this?

Which scripture?

The next problem is to locate the passage to which "as the scripture hath said" refers and, if it could be identified, it might throw light on the correct rendering of verse 38. In fact, there appears

2   Brown, *loc cit*, page 319.
3   *ibid*.
4   Bruce, F. F. (1983) *The Gospel of John*, Eerdmans, page 181.

to be no scripture in the Hebrew Old Testament or the Greek Septuagint (LXX) that matches this saying. There are, however, several passages that could be said to parallel the concept, and it has been suggested that the phrase is not recounting a specific verse but rather encapsulating the essence of these scriptures. We may discount the verses from the apocryphal books that have been suggested by some commentators for, although they provide evidence of the linguistic equation of 'flowing water' and 'spirit', it seems improbable that the Lord would refer to uninspired texts.

One passage which may qualify is Exodus 17 where Moses, on striking the rock, produced copious amounts of flowing water:

"And the LORD said unto Moses, Pass on before the people, and take with thee of the elders of Israel; and thy rod, wherewith thou smotest the river, take in thy hand, and go. Behold, I will stand before thee there upon the rock in Horeb; and thou shalt smite the rock, and there shall come water out of it, that the people may drink."   (verses 5,6)

This incident is reiterated in Deuteronomy 8:

"… the LORD thy God, who brought thee forth out of the land of Egypt, out of the house of bondage; who led thee through the great and terrible wilderness … and thirsty ground where was no water; who brought thee forth water out of the rock of flint …"   (verses 14,15)

Perhaps the account closest to the passage in John is Psalm 78:

"He clave rocks in the wilderness, and gave them drink abundantly as out of the depths. He brought streams also out of the rock, and caused waters to run down like rivers."   (verses 15,16)

This incident is also mentioned in Psalm 105:

"He opened the rock, and *waters gushed out*; they ran in the dry places *like a river*."   (verse 41)

And Psalm 114:

"Tremble, thou earth, at the presence of the Lord, at the presence of the God of Jacob, who turned the rock into a pool of water, the flint into a fountain of waters."   (verses 7,8)

Psalm 114 was one of those sung in the processions by the Jews during the Feast of Tabernacles, the very time when the Lord Jesus made this puzzling pronouncement.[5]

The water from the rock event is also mentioned in three passages in Isaiah:

"Behold, I will do a new thing; now shall it spring forth; shall ye not know it? I will even make a way in the wilderness, and rivers in the desert ... I give waters in the wilderness, and rivers in the desert, to give drink to my people, my chosen: the people which I formed for myself, that they might set forth my praise." (43:19-21)

"... with a voice of singing declare ye, tell this, utter it even to the end of the earth: say ye, The LORD hath redeemed his servant Jacob. And they thirsted not when he led them through the deserts; he caused the waters to flow out of the rock for them; he clave the rock also, and the waters gushed out." (48:20,21)

Of these passages, Isaiah 44 is particularly appropriate:

"Yet now hear, O Jacob my servant, and Israel, who I have chosen: Thus saith the LORD that made thee, and formed thee from the womb, who will help thee: Fear not, O Jacob my servant; and thou, Jeshurun, whom I have chosen. For I will pour water upon him that is thirsty, and streams upon the dry ground; *I will pour my Spirit upon thy seed*, and my blessing upon thine offspring." (verses 1-3)

Given the number of occasions it is recounted in the Old Testament, this incident is evidently highly significant. In 1 Corinthians, Paul explains that this, along with other aspects of the wilderness journey, was actually a prefiguring of Christ:

"For I would not, brethren, have you ignorant, that our fathers were all under the cloud, and all passed through the sea; and were all baptized unto Moses in the cloud and in the sea; and did all eat the same spiritual meat; and did all drink the same

---

5   Guilding, A. (1960) *The Fourth Gospel and Jewish Worship*, Clarendon Press, page 103.

spiritual drink: for they drank of a spiritual rock that followed them: and *the rock was Christ*."   (1 Corinthians 10:1-4)

Here we have the explanation of the Lord's remarks. The context is the Feast of Tabernacles which not only reminded Israel of the time when, in their wilderness journey they lived in temporary shelter, but also of the time when copious amounts of water flowed from the smitten rock, prefiguring the flow of the Spirit from that one which the rock signified – the Lord Jesus Christ.

Some commentators have also drawn a parallel with the water flowing from the millennial temple which increases as it flows, even though no tributaries are described (Ezekiel 47:1-12); and also the divided stream, flowing both into the Dead Sea and the Mediterranean, described in Zechariah 14:8. However, these are literal rivers of the future, whereas this passage draws the analogy between the literal life-giving river derived from the smitten rock in the wilderness and the life-giving Spirit derived from the Lord himself.

The psalmist who composed Psalm 46 describes a river, which is more than a water supply. It also has a spiritual dimension that brings joy:

"There is a river, the streams whereof make glad the city of God, the holy place of the tabernacles of the Most High. God is in the midst of her; she shall not be moved: God will help her, and that right early."   (verses 4,5)

SUMMARY

The identity of the one from whom the rivers of water will flow, figuratively representing the Holy Spirit, is the Lord Jesus. The reference to scripture is not specifically to a quotable verse but to the general sense of several scriptures. The incident of Moses striking the rock in the wilderness, causing water to flow copiously, is cited in several Psalms and in Isaiah. Paul refers to the event in 1 Corinthians and concludes with the statement that "the rock was Christ".

"In my Father's house are many mansions ..."
(John 14:2)

I N his book *Wrested Scriptures* (page 191), the late Brother Ron Abel, having stated that a mansion, by definition, is larger than a house, posed the question: "How then can one have mansions in a house?"

It might be supposed that this passage is hyperbolic, that is, an exaggeration which is not to be taken literally, in order to stress the ample accommodation available in God's house, which is so generous that it amounts to a 'mansion'. However, reference to the original Greek text shows that this view is not tenable.

"Many rooms"
The confusion arises from the KJV translation of the original Greek μοναι, *monai*, as "mansions", which goes back to Tyndale, who derived it from the Latin *'mansiones'* of the Vulgate version. Apparently, ancient itineraries listed the places where one would stay overnight (*mansiones*)[1] and also the places where the horses were changed (*mutates*).

The original word is only found in this chapter, here and verse 23. The Greek *monai* (plural) simply means 'dwellings' or 'abiding-places'. It is echoed later in the chapter at verse 23 where the Lord explains that he and his Father will come to those who keep his word and make their *abode* (singular) with them.

Reference to a more modern translation immediately solves the puzzle. For example, the RSV reads, "In my Father's

[1] Cf. B. F. Westcott (1958) *The Gospel of St. John*, page 200.

house are many *rooms*", as does the NIV and the ESV. In verse 23 these versions have "and make our *home* with him". Interestingly, the NEB, which so often uses quite modern expressions, uses the slightly more archaic "dwelling-places" and "dwelling", respectively.

Here is a case where the beloved KJV fails us, as the translators in the seventeenth century clearly wished to retain the Tyndale rendering, as did the revisers in 1880 when they published the RV, although they did include a marginal reference "Or, abiding-places".

Some commentators stress that it is unfortunate that "mansions" was used here, since in ancient times these were places of temporary accommodation for travellers, quite inappropriate for the context.[2] Others draw attention to the fact that in New Testament times, houses were often enlarged to provide for the extended family and hence may have had many rooms. In Roman cities, houses were usually of multiple occupancy, equivalent to our tower blocks[3] and would, therefore, have many rooms.

Looking at the context

Although this verse is often quoted during the funerals of other denominations, generally in association with an assertion that the deceased is now in heaven, it is evident that the passage cannot be construed in this way. As is so often the case, verses are cited without any reference to the context. In verse 2, the words "I go to prepare a place for you" are followed by the assurance, "And if I go ... I will come again, and receive you".

We are privileged to understand the true meaning of the Lord's words. God's first house was destroyed by the Babylonians

---

2   For example, J.H. Bernard (1928) *A Critical and Exegetical Commentary on the Gospel according to St. John*, ICC, pages 531-533, demonstrates that the word must mean "abodes or permanent dwelling-places, not merely temporary stations on a journey".

3   B. Milne (1993) *The Message of John, The Bible Speaks Today*, page 210 says, "For today's urban dweller, 'In my Father's apartment block are many apartments' would be possible as a translation".

and the second would soon be demolished by the Romans, but God's real house would be eternal:

> "So then ye are no more strangers and sojourners, but ye are fellow-citizens with the saints, and of the household of God, being built upon the foundation of the apostles and prophets, Christ Jesus himself being the chief corner stone; in whom each several building, fitly framed together, groweth into a holy temple in the Lord; in whom ye also are builded together for a habitation of God in the Spirit."   (Ephesians 2:19-22)

David, who was forbidden to construct the house he so longed to build for God, appreciated that while God would build him a "house" (that is, a dynasty, 2 Samuel 7:11) and although Solomon his son would build the temple, his distant descendant (2 Samuel 7:19) would build the permanent spiritual house. Here, expressed in the words of one of our lovely hymns (12), based on David's Psalm 23:6, is the aspiration of every faithful disciple: "… and in God's house, for evermore, my dwelling-place shall be".

SUMMARY

Part of the problem here is the use of words, the meaning of which have changed over the centuries. A 'mansion' today is usually regarded as a larger building than a house, but originally it was simply a stopping place on an itinerary. A modern rendering of the Lord's phrase would be, "In my Father's house are many rooms".

"The net ... full of great fishes, a hundred and fifty-three ..."
(John 21:11)

T HERE is no puzzle in the statement that, when the net was hauled to land, it contained 153 large fishes. The difficulty is whether this has any significance and, if so, what is it? Some commentators are convinced that it must be significant, otherwise why would John have recorded it? It is equally noteworthy that the trouble was taken to count the catch, which also suggests that some importance was attached to the number. It is a sound maxim of scripture study, always to consider that God is unlikely to waste words and, when details are provided, they are invariably important. Through the centuries a large number of commentators, believing that the number is not merely incidental, have attempted to explain its significance, while others have dismissed the suggestion. As an example of the latter position, Professor Hunter[1] wrote: "In our view, the 153 fish are no more symbolical than the hundred yards that Peter swam. It is the remembered number of a 'bumper' catch". In fact, the NEB text states that the distance was *about* a hundred yards" (in Greek, 200 cubits) but that is an *approximation*, while the number of fishes is given *exactly*.

Ingenious suggestions
What then is the significance? One can only marvel at the variety and ingenuity of suggestions, especially when, as will be described

---

1   Hunter, A. M. (1965) *The Gospel according to John*, The Cambridge Bible Commentary on the New English Bible, page 95.

below, the best explanation is the simplest. For example, it has been claimed that ancient zoologists considered that there were 153 kinds of fishes and so this catch represented the universality of the Gospel. In reality, there are at least 32,000 fish species so the ancient inventory was rather inadequate.

Examples of the extent to which ingenuity has been exercised on this puzzle, have been described by Carson,[2] based on the use of gematria, that is, the substitution of the numerical values of letters in a word and then adding these to obtain the total. In both Hebrew and Greek there were no symbols for numbers corresponding to our Arabic numerals. For example, in Greek α *alpha* = 1, β *beta* = 2 and so on.[3] The Romans similarly used letters for numbers but these were assigned to only a few values. For example, the Romans used v for 5, x for 10, c for 100, m for 1,000. Numbers were made by combining the letters so that, for example, xv = 15. In Hebrew, by adding up the values of each letter in a word, the total formed its gematria. In Ezekiel 47 we read:

> "And it shall come to pass, that every living creature which swarmeth, in every place whither the rivers come, shall live; and there shall be a very great multitude of fish; for these waters are come thither, and the waters of the sea shall be healed, and everything shall live whithersoever the river cometh. And it shall come to pass, that fishers shall stand by it: from En-gedi even unto En-eglaim shall be a place for the spreading of nets; their fish shall be after their kinds, as the fish of the great sea, exceeding many."   (Ezekiel 47:9,10)

The emphasis on "a very great multitude of fish" in verse 9 and "exceeding many" of verse 10 has parallels with John 21. The gematria of the key place names En-gedi and En-eglaim are 17 and 153, respectively. The number 153 is the sum of the first 17 integers, that is, 1+2+3...+17. While this might seem an

2   Carson, D. A. (1991) *The Gospel According to John*, The Pillar New Testament Commentary, page 672.

3   Bullinger, E. W. (1894 / 1967) *Number in Scripture, Its Supernatural Design and Spiritual Significance*, pages 48,49.

interesting coincidence, it seems highly improbable that the readers of John's Gospel would make this connection, especially the Jews of the Diaspora and the Gentiles whose knowledge of Hebrew would be limited. Even if they did, what is its significance?

Peter Owen[4] linked this number to Jacob's blessing of Ephraim and Manasseh, which included their descendants growing into a multitude, noting that 'grow' was also rendered in the KJV margin, "as fishes do increase" (Genesis 48:16). Thus, when this is substituted, the phrase would become: "Let them, as fishes do increase, become a multitude." He also noted that the word "multitude" is used 153 times in scripture. His conclusion is that those "who enter into covenant relationship with God will be drawn out of the turbulence of this sinful world to the safety of the sea shore". The majority of other translations have "grow" (RV, RSV, Jerusalem, NEB, NIV, and Young's Literal Translation) and do not corroborate the KJV margin reading, but the marginal reading of the ESV ("Or *let them be like fish for multitude*") is close, as are also the notes in *The Companion Bible*. The Tanakh text is "may they be teeming multitudes ..." which approaches this sense. It may also be significant that the Hebrew word does not occur elsewhere. Once more, however, apart from the simile of the abundance or fecundity of fish, how does this assist our understanding of the significance of the number 153?

Bullinger[5] has provided a comprehensive review of the various solutions offered in the past and provides a list of scripture passages where individuals received direct blessings from Christ. The total number of these individuals is 153.

Another suggestion involves the gematria of the phrase "sons of God" in Hebrew (*B^eni ha-elohim*) but 153 can only be derived if the definite article is included. This has been linked to the "sons of God" in Genesis and the suggestion offered that the "fishers of men" are to take the "gospel message to the

---

4   Owen, P. (2013) *153 Fishes*, Testimony 83, page 98.
5   Bullinger, E. W. (1894) *Number in Scripture*, pages 273-278.

whole world".[6] This Hebrew phrase is, however, capable of other translations (see Puzzling Passage No. 2).

It has been noted that the gematria of the Greek word for fishes (*ichthues*) gives 1,224 which is 153 × 8. Thus "fishes" suggests those that are caught in the Gospel net according to the eighth sign".[7] The problem here is that "fishes" in John 21:8,11 is ιχθυων, *ichthyōn* and in verse 10 'οψαριον, *opsarion*, with gematria of 1,329 and 992, respectively.

Ingenuity knows no bounds in attempting to solve this puzzle. It has been noted that the number of fishes in the catch that day was actually 154, since the Lord was already cooking fish (verse 9). There were seven disciples (verse 2) present so there would be 22 each, the same number as the letters in the Hebrew alphabet and books in the Hebrew scriptures. The conclusion is drawn that the "disciples now have the complete word of God ... from which to teach" and "if we go fishing for people for Christ, it will be profitable only if the Lord's advice is followed ... remembering that he is the one who does the calling – the one who caught the first fish".[8]

Others have noted the unusual mathematical attributes of 153. For example, the cubes of the three numbers ($1^3+5^3+3^3$) add up to 153! Many have observed that 153 is a triangular number[9] and also that several other numbers in the New Testament are triangular numbers, including 120 (Acts 1:15); 276 (Acts 27:37) and 666 (Revelation 13:18). While this is unlikely to be a coincidence, again we may reasonably ask, 'What significance does this have for our understanding of the incident in John 21:11'? Carson[10] concludes his review by noting that if John "has some symbolism in mind ... he has hidden it well". It would be more accurate to say that the obsession of commentators with

6   Cox, P. (2013) *153 Fishes*, Testimony 83, page 277.
7   Whittaker, H. A. (1989) *Studies in the Gospels*, page 830.
8   Simons, A. (2014) *153 Fishes*, Testimony 84, page 147.
9   Whittaker, H. A. (1969) *He is Risen Indeed*, page 78.
10 Carson, D. A. (1991) *The Gospel According to John*, The Pillar New Testament Commentary, page 673.

the actual numerical value has obscured their consideration of its relevance in context.

The significance of context

One might reasonably assume that the significance of this number is related to the context of the passage. It begins with Peter's comment: "I go a fishing" (verse 3). He had, however, been informed by the Lord Jesus that this was not to be his, or his brother Andrew's, future vocation:

> "And he saith unto them, Come ye after me, and I will make you fishers of men. And they straightway left the nets, and followed him."   (Matthew 4:19,20)

Why Peter decided to go back to his earlier trade as a fisherman is not revealed, but it seems probable that he and the others had time on their hands between the appearances of the risen Lord and possibly, given their apparently strange behaviour when he did appear (John 21:12), they had not yet fully come to terms with their new situation.

Peter's experience was a reiteration of his earlier encounter with the Lord. The healing of his mother-in-law seemed to have little impact (Matthew 8:14,15) but when this expert fisherman, having toiled all night and caught nothing, realised that the carpenter from the hill-top town of Nazareth knew exactly where the nets should be cast, and the resulting catch was sufficient to swamp the boat, he knelt down and said, "Depart from me; for I am a sinful man, O Lord" (Luke 5:8).

It is probable that the Lord was teaching another tangible lesson to Peter and the other disciples. We learn from Acts 1:15 that the number of disciples in Jerusalem at this time was about 120. After a three-and-a-half-year ministry, when thousands flocked to hear the Lord, this is a disappointingly small final 'catch'. Of course, there were signs that many in his audience became disillusioned. Even the disciples seemed ready to desert him and he asked, "Will ye also go away?" (John 6:67, KJV). It was Peter who rallied them with his realistic comment, asking where could they possibly go since the Lord had the words of eternal life?

Now Peter was to become truly a fisher of men. The catch of 153 large fishes was only a foretaste of what was to be. It is surely significant that the net was filled with large fish (21:11), perhaps indicating that these were those disciples whose faith was strong and who never doubted that Jesus was indeed the Christ. With 120 in Jerusalem and, presumably, thirty-three who had remained in Galilee, the fisherman whose catch totalled 153 would now change his vocation and become the shepherd who would feed the Lord's sheep and lambs (verses 15-17).

It might be thought that Paul's list of the post-resurrection appearances of the Lord Jesus in 1 Corinthians might undermine this suggestion for he says:

"... and that he appeared to Cephas; then to the twelve; then he appeared to above five hundred brethren at once, of whom the greater part remain until now, but some are fallen asleep; then he appeared to James; then to all the apostles ..."

(1 Corinthians 15:5-7)

It seems highly likely that once the Lord's resurrection had been attested, the word would spread rapidly amongst many of those disciples who deserted the Lord, as recorded in John 6:66, and they would return. During one of their assemblies the Lord confirmed the apostles' affirmation by appearing in person. His subsequent appearance to James would be to James the Lord's brother and "the apostles" presumably means more than "the twelve" who are mentioned after Peter.

Within a short time the Jerusalem contingent would be augmented by 3,000 (Acts 2:41) and later still by 5,000 men (Acts 4:4). The miracles that were performed at the hands of the apostles fulfilled the Lord's prophecy that they would perform greater works than the Lord himself (John 14:12).

From this significant but numerable catch would develop a community contributing to an ultimate total that, at the Lord's return, would be as many as the stars in heaven and the sand on earth (Hebrews 11:12).

SUMMARY

Although many complex and even ingenious solutions to the significance of the catch of 153 large fishes have been proposed, the simplest and most reasonable is given by the context, that is, Peter's return to actual fishing, when he should be a "fisher of men". The catch of 153 fishes represents the number of the disciples remaining faithful after the Lord's death and resurrection. The number in Jerusalem is given as 120 (Acts 1:15) and it would be reasonable to assume that the other thirty-three were in Galilee. When the reality of the resurrection was known, many disciples who had earlier forsaken the Lord (John 6:66) returned (1 Corinthians 15:6). After Pentecost, Peter's 'fishing' produced 'catches' numbering thousands.

"Saved; yet so as by fire ..."
(1 Corinthians 3:15)

T HE context of this passage is the description of the Christian community in Corinth as "God's husbandry ... God's building".

With reference to the former, Paul 'planted' the community and later Apollos ensured its growth by 'watering' it. The analogy is then transferred from agriculture to the construction of a building. Paul stresses that God equipped him with the necessary skills and as a "wise masterbuilder" he laid the foundations of the Corinthian Ecclesia and others subsequently built upon these. He stresses that the sure foundations, resting on the rock of Christ (Matthew 7:24), determined the shape of the building that would be erected. The Greek text implies that no other foundation could be laid "alongside", in other words, there was no way to begin again (or construct an extension on a different foundation).

Paul also used the analogy of a building, and of a temple in particular, to describe the ecclesia in his Ephesian letter. He says that they –

"... are built upon the foundation of the apostles and prophets, Jesus Christ himself being the chief corner stone; in whom all the building fitly framed together groweth unto an holy temple in the Lord: in whom ye also are builded together for an habitation of God through the Spirit."

(Ephesians 2:20-22)[1]

---

1   Quotations in this chapter are from the KJV unless otherwise indicated.

In writing to Corinth he describes the ecclesia there as "God's building", which, as a wise master-builder he had erected on a sound foundation, that is, the Lord Jesus Christ (1 Corinthians 3:9-11). Others had now begun to erect an edifice on this foundation, and Paul warned it was essential that attention should be paid as to how the building was to be erected and the materials to be used.

Care in building

In particular, he drew attention to the sorts of building materials which might be used, citing gold, silver, precious stones, wood, hay and stubble. The first three materials in the list are extremely durable and very costly and, therefore, especially appropriate for a fine permanent building such as a temple. They were used to great effect in that built by Solomon, which was "exceeding magnifical". David was forbidden to build the temple but prepared the materials, as he explained:

"Now I have prepared with all my might for the house of my God the gold for things to be made of gold, and the silver for things of silver, and the brass for things of brass, the iron for things of iron, and wood for things of wood; onyx stones, and stones to be set, glistering stones, and of divers colours, and all manner of precious stones, and marble stones in abundance." (1 Chronicles 29:2; cf. 22:14-16)

The temple built by Herod was "adorned with goodly stones and gifts" (Luke 21:5) as were the temples of Greece and Rome.

The last three materials in Paul's list, namely wood, hay and stubble are relatively inexpensive, of limited durability and are, above all, prone to ready combustion. This is particularly relevant to the construction of dwellings in Roman cities. Although at street level stone or brick was often used, the upper storeys (cf. Acts 20:9) were built of wooden framework and the walls made from stubble mixed with mud and the roof might be thatched.[2] Where buildings were close together, a fire that

---

2   Mare, W. H. (1976) *1 Corinthians*, The Expositor's Bible Commentary, Vol. 10, page 207.

started on the ground or lower floors would spread quickly upwards and then across narrow streets to adjacent buildings. Modern fire appliances are sometimes inadequate to cope with fires but in ancient times the situation was frequently hopeless. "The supreme test for a building in a Hellenistic city was fire."[3]

Paul's warning about the need to exercise great care in building is seen to be vital when he goes on to explain that the test of its quality will come when the building is subjected to fire. Fire was just as devastating in the ancient world as it is today. As James remarks, "Behold, how great a matter a little fire kindleth!" (James 3:5).

A building constructed entirely of stone and embellished with silver and gold would readily withstand the effects of fire. There would hardly be anything to contribute to the fire. Even if the gold and silver melted, they would not be destroyed. On the other hand, a building made from wood, and thatched with hay and stubble would rapidly burn to the ground.

It may be significant that both types of building would be constructed on the same foundation plan but only one will continue to maintain the outline of the plan above ground after the fire.

The test of fire

What is the reality to which Paul's analogy refers? Paul's lesson is directed to those who were corrupting true doctrine[4] and causing factions (1 Corinthians 1:11,12) in the Corinthian Ecclesia, rather than edifying. It may have seemed soundly built, but in reality it was wood, hay and stubble. The Day of Judgement would reveal its true nature. Two consequences would follow from what the fire revealed:

---

3   Garland, D. E., *1 Corinthians*, Baker Exegetical Commentary on the New Testament, page 118.
4   For example: tolerating unacceptable morality 1 Corinthians 5:1-13; unacceptable behaviour at the breaking of bread (11:20-29); misuse of Spirit gifts (14:1-33) and denial of the reality of resurrection (15:12-23).

"If any man's work abide which he hath built thereupon, he shall receive a reward. If any man's work shall be burned, he shall suffer loss: but he himself shall be saved; yet so as by fire."   (1 Corinthians 3:14,15)

A construction which withstood the conflagration and remained unharmed would demonstrate that its builder had built wisely and would bring reward in the approval of the Lord. One which failed and was destroyed would demonstrate the inadequacy of the builder and his construction: he would suffer loss in the sense that his labours would have been in vain and would not receive commendation. The one responsible would, however, escape with his life – "yet so as by fire". This latter phrase is generally reckoned to be proverbial, equivalent to 'by the skin of his teeth'.

Individual responsibility

Paul describes the ecclesia as a temple of God (verse 16) and those who defiled it would themselves be defiled (KJV, "destroyed") by God (verse 17). Earlier in the chapter Paul has emphasised that those who laboured to build the ecclesia had an individual responsibility to work with and not against the will of God and consequently, "every man shall receive his own reward according to his own labour" (verse 8).

The leaders of each community are those who "must give account" of their stewardship (Hebrews 13:17). It is possible to build an ecclesia of sorts on the basis of worldly wisdom, popular feeling, contemporary fashion, sentimentality, optional involvement and even indifference. But its true nature will "be made manifest, for the day [the day of the Lord] shall declare it". The exhortation is clear: "Let all things be done unto edifying" (1 Corinthians 14:26).

SUMMARY

Paul described the ecclesia at Corinth as "God's building" and although he had laid the firm spiritual foundation (Christ), others were now building on this and he was concerned that the edifice would meet the necessary spiritual standards (gold, silver and precious stones) and not sub-standard (wood, hay and stubble). The Day of Judgment would reveal its quality. Just as buildings in Roman times survived fire quite well when they were made of largely non-combustible materials (stone, brick and tiles) and the thatched wooden buildings were totally destroyed, so the spiritual quality of the ecclesia would become evident at the Lord's return. The builder in both cases would escape the conflagration but building with wood, hay and stubble would mean that his labour had been in vain. On the other hand, the builder whose construction survived the fiery test would be commended.

"Deliver such an one unto Satan ..."
(1 Corinthians 5:5)

P AUL, having castigated the Corinthians for tolerating gross immorality in their midst, declares how the culprit should be treated:

"For I verily, being absent in body but present in spirit, have already as though I were present judged him that hath so wrought this thing, in the name of our Lord Jesus, ye being gathered together, and my spirit, with the power of our Lord Jesus, to deliver such a one unto Satan for the destruction of the flesh, that the spirit may be saved in the day of the Lord Jesus." (1 Corinthians 5:3-5, ASV)

There is a similar statement in 1 Timothy, where Paul exhorts Timothy to live up to the potential which was indicated by earlier prophecy and notes how two disciples failed to do this and were punished:

"This charge I commit unto thee, my child Timothy, according to the prophecies which led the way to thee, that by them thou mayest war the good warfare; holding faith and a good conscience; which some having thrust from them made shipwreck concerning the faith: of whom is Hymenaeus and Alexander; whom I delivered unto Satan, that they might be taught not to blaspheme." (1 Timothy 1:18-20, ASV)

Whatever these passages mean, they are a clear indication that the conventional view of a 'personal' devil, who is intent on undermining faith and opposing God, is untenable. In the first passage 'delivering to Satan' is for the express purpose of saving the individual, while in the second it would be strange if the Satan of orthodoxy was giving lessons in how not to blaspheme!

Satan

'Satan' is derived from Hebrew and simply means an adversary, for good or for evil; the word itself is neutral in this respect. It is sometimes plural, which also runs counter to conventional belief. Adversaries take many forms, including angels (Numbers 22:22; Job 1:6); hostile neighbouring countries (1 Kings 5:4; 11:14,23); political enemies (1 Samuel 29:4) and personal enemies (Psalm 38:20; 71:13; 109:4,29).

It has been suggested by some commentators[1] that "delivering unto Satan" means condemning at least to illness and more probably to death. There are precedents in the blindness of Elymas (Acts 13:8-12) and the deaths of Ananias and Sapphira (Acts 5:5,10). However, it is difficult to understand how death will result in the individual's salvation in the day of the Lord.

Paul's "thorn in the flesh", which is described as a "messenger of satan" (2 Corinthians 12:7), might have been a distressing illness or an eye problem to which he seems to refer in Galatians 4:

"I bear you witness, that, if possible, ye would have plucked out your eyes and given them to me."   (verse 15)

However, as Paul was steeped in the Old Testament, it is likely that his reference to a thorn in the flesh is an allusion to Numbers 33:

"But if ye will not drive out the inhabitants of the land from before you; then it shall come to pass, that those which ye let remain of them shall be pricks in your eyes, and thorns in your sides, and shall vex you in the land wherein ye dwell."

(Numbers 33:55, KJV)

Here it is the pagan remnant that is a potential 'thorn in the flesh' to Israel. How ironic then that the opposition of Jews to the Gospel is seen by Paul in the same light!

---

1   See, for example, the review in Fee, G. (1987) *The First Epistle to the Corinthians*, page 210 (although he does not concur with this view); and Thiselton, A. C. (2000) *The First Epistle to the Corinthians*, page 397.

Jewish opposition

So, once more we have the adversary identified as the Jewish opponents to Paul's preaching. He accepted the Lord's assurance that his grace was sufficient and wrote:

"... Most gladly therefore will I rather glory in my infirmities, that the power of Christ may rest upon me. Therefore I take pleasure in infirmities, in reproaches, in necessities, in persecutions, in distresses for Christ's sake: for when I am weak, then am I strong."   (2 Corinthians 12:9,10, KJV)

The theme of opposition recurs in Paul's writings. Paul wrote to Timothy regarding the appropriate conduct for younger sisters, as follows:

"I will therefore that the younger women marry, bear children, guide the house, give none occasion to the adversary to speak reproachfully. For some are already turned aside after Satan."
(1 Timothy 5:14,15, KJV)

Here the two ideas, "the adversary" and "satan" are linked together. The adversary or satan here is clearly those who oppose Christians and who will use any misconduct against them. The most likely candidates are the hostile Jews, although Gentiles may also be implicated.

Problems in Thessalonica

In writing to the Thessalonians Paul apologised for not having returned after his rapid departure following the riots (Acts 17:5-9):

"But we, brethren, being taken from you for a short time in presence, not in heart, endeavoured the more abundantly to see your face with great desire. Wherefore we would have come unto you, even I Paul, once and again; but Satan hindered us."
(1 Thessalonians 2:17,18, KJV)

Paul could not return to Thessalonica while Jason and the other disciples were bound over to keep the peace (Acts 17:9), since this would almost certainly result in further riots and expose his friends to even greater danger. Once again, it is evident that the opposition to Paul is the combination of Jewish adversaries and the Roman authorities.

We may now have some idea of what "delivering to satan" may mean. It could be the imposition of an unpleasant illness which might bring the offender to their senses. It could mean disfellowship, which would place the offender back in the world where they might better appreciate the blessings of the Truth. These two possibilities would be appropriate for Hymenaeus and Alexander.

In the case of the brother whose gross immorality was "not so much as named among the Gentiles" (KJV) or "not tolerated even among pagans" (ESV),[2] we understand that such conduct was illegal under both Jewish and Roman law.[3] Could it be then, that Paul was instructing the Corinthians not to shelter such a brother but to allow the authorities to deal with him according to law? This would make it abundantly clear to all that Christians would not tolerate behaviour which was condemned even by the licentious world of Corinth. The brother, having suffered whatever punishment was meted out would, one hopes, see the error of his ways.[4]

Paul's intention was not primarily to punish but to save. This is the true spirit of Christian love (cf. Hebrews 12:5-11). The treatment may sometimes have to be harsh but this is one case where the end does justify the means.

SUMMARY

'Satan' is derived from Hebrew and simply means 'adversary', whether for good or ill. To deliver someone to satan may take several forms, but in the case of the man who was guilty of gross immorality it would probably mean not sheltering him but handing him over to the authorities for trial and consequent punishment.

---

2   Lit. "as is not even among the Gentiles", as in the RV.
3   See Fee *loc. cit.* page 200 and Thiselton, *loc. cit.* page 385.
4   It is not certain that 2 Corinthians 2:6 is a reference to the case in 1 Corinthians 5:1.

Manumission or not?
(1 Corinthians 7:21)

THIS puzzling passage, relating to manumission, that is, the granting of freedom to slaves, is, in the ASV and RV margin: "Wast thou called being a bondservant? Care not for it: nay, even if thou canst become free, use it rather." Other versions render this differently, as is discussed below.

The problems with this passage are twofold: it is ambiguous in the original Greek, which has led to a variety of translations, and it is rather odd in its context, given the procedures for freeing slaves in the first century.

Slavery in the Roman Empire

In New Testament times, in the urban areas at least a third of the total population was enslaved.[1] Originally, slaves were prisoners of war or a result of abduction, often by pirates. Over time the origin changed, partly because the extent of Roman conquests decreased but mainly because the children produced by female slaves were sufficient to maintain the slave population. Such children were automatically slaves and became the property of the slave-owner. In addition, some sold themselves into slavery; others were simply captured and put up for sale in the slave-markets. This is the meaning of the term "men-stealers" in 1 Timothy 1:10 (KJV / RV), also translated as "kidnappers" (NKJV), "slave-traders" (NIV), "enslavers" (ESV). Although

---

1   See Bartchy, S. S. (1992) in: *The Anchor Bible Dictionary*, Vol. 6, pages 65-73 for a comprehensive account of slavery in the Greco-Roman world.

slavery itself is not condemned in scripture, to include this occupation in the list of characteristics and activities that should not apply to those in Christ indicates how widespread it was.

Slaves were not considered as people but as things, merely chattels to be owned and used as their owners thought fit, "to be bought and sold like any other animal".[2] Their condition was entirely dependent on the attitude and status of their owners: some would be treated well, others quite badly. The financial value of slaves was the only factor that guaranteed some level of care, for a weak and sickly slave would fetch a low price. Those employed in agriculture, mining and galley-ships suffered severe hardships while others might enjoy a relatively good life as doctors, teachers, administrators, secretaries and similar professions. Those in this latter group were extremely valuable. It is possible that Erastus, the "city treasurer" or *aedile*, mentioned in Romans 16:23, had 'sold' himself to the city of Corinth in order to obtain this important office, yet was wealthy enough to pay for the pavement that can be seen in Corinth today.[3] If this is correct, we have someone who was legally a slave of the city and yet also a wealthy "treasurer" of the provincial capital, Corinth.

Slaves had few legal rights. One was the ability to call on the services of a friend of their master to intercede on their behalf. Onesimus availed himself of this right when Paul interceded with Philemon on his behalf (Philemon 10,17,18). On the other hand, slaves who absconded could be treated harshly when recaptured. They were often branded with a letter 'F' on their foreheads to indicate that they had been fugitives and made to wear a collar indicating their owner's name and address and the reward for their return, in much the same way as dog owners do today. Paul seems to have anticipated this problem when he wrote, "For this perhaps is why he was parted from you for a while (literally, 'an hour'), that you might have him back forever" (Philemon 15, ESV), thereby implying that Onesimus had not

2 Brunt, P. A. (1987) "Labour" in: *The Roman World*, Vol. II, J. Wacher (Ed.), page 705.
3 See Hellawell, J. M. (2014) *Beginning at Jerusalem*, page 238 and Plate 17.

really absconded but simply 'popped out' for an hour! Returning runaway slaves was a legal obligation, with which Paul in effect complied. Sometimes slaves were abducted in order that the reward could be claimed on returning them to their owners.

One particularly horrible law required that when slaves were examined as witnesses their evidence had to be obtained under torture. For this reason some slave owners would free their slaves in order that they could not be tortured into reporting the misdemeanours of their masters. This brings us to the subject of manumitted slaves who were then known as freedmen or freedwomen.

Freedmen and freedwomen

Paul refers to the status of freedmen in 1 Corinthians 7, where he explained that slaves and free have their spiritual, if not legal, status changed when they become Christians:

> "For he that was called in the Lord being a bondservant, is the Lord's freedman: likewise he that was called, being free, is Christ's bondservant. Ye were bought with a price; become not bondservants of men." (1 Corinthians 7:22,23)

The free individual has been bought, just as slaves were, by Christ and become his bondservant, but the slave has, at least on the eternal scale, gained true freedom in Christ.

Granting slaves their freedom was relatively common. Sometimes it was given in return for faithful service or occurred when the slave-owner died. Some owners might free a female slave in order to marry her. Manumission was normally given when men reached the age of thirty years and women at twenty. These ages coincide with Roman life expectancy at birth but, after high infant mortality, at age ten a Roman would have a life expectancy of another thirty-five years or so. Older slaves would have a low value and an owner may consider that it was better to free them than continue to support them.

The significant factors in manumission were that it was the owner's prerogative as to whether a slave would be freed and although a freed slave's status changed from being a 'thing' to being a human being, freedom might have constraints imposed. Freed slaves often adopted the family names of their owners. Usually slaves would continue to provide some service to their former masters and there might be a legally binding contract attached to the manumission. The continued connection could be advantageous because freed slaves might have no ready means of supporting themselves. Educated slaves, however, were often able to utilise their skills to advantage and achieve considerable status. It is noteworthy that the governor Felix (Acts 23:25,26) was a freed slave who rose to high office.

Paul's advice

The problem with Paul's advice in 1 Corinthians 7:21 is, what does "use it rather" mean? Does it mean, 'Don't be concerned that you are a slave but if there is an opportunity to gain your freedom, take it'? Or, does it mean, 'Even if you are presented with the opportunity to gain your freedom, don't avail yourself of it; on the contrary, remain a slave and use this status to demonstrate your Christian faith to your master'?

This latter meaning would be equivalent to the possibility under the Law where a slave who loved his master did not avail himself of the release:

"But if the servant shall plainly say, I love my master, my wife, and my children; I will not go out free: then his master shall bring him unto God, and shall bring him to the door, or unto the door-post; and his master shall bore his ear through with an awl; and he shall serve him for ever."   (Exodus 21:5,6)

Translators are divided as to which is the correct meaning of Paul's phrase, largely because the original Greek is ambiguous. Some versions, for example the KJV and RV are neutral and simply maintain the ambiguity. However the RV margin offers exactly the opposite of the main text:

"Wast thou called being a bondservant? Care not for it: nay, *even if* thou canst become free, use it rather."

This reading was adopted by the American Revisers (ASV). The NKJV also preserves the ambiguity:

"Were you called while a slave? Do not be concerned about it; but if you can be made free, rather use it."

Other versions suggest the opposite, for example the NIV:

"Were you a slave when you were called? Don't let it trouble you – although if you can gain your freedom, do so."

The NASB, the NLT and Moffatt take it this way as does the NEB and the REB in the text:

"Were you a slave when you were called? Do not let that trouble you: but if a chance of liberty should come, take it."

However the margin gives the exact opposite sense and reads:

"Were you a slave when you were called? Do not let that trouble you: but *even* if a chance of liberty should come, *choose rather to make good use of your servitude.*"

The context seems to imply that the slave should not accept freedom, for verse 20 is clear enough: everyone should remain in the same state on becoming a disciple:

"Let every man abide in the same calling wherein he was called." (1 Corinthians 7:20, KJV)

Verse 22, in which Paul explains the change in status in Christ, seems to harmonise with this by implying that, since in Christ "there can be neither bond nor free ..." (Galatians 3:28; cf. 1 Corinthians 12:13) worldly status is of no consequence.

What are we to conclude regarding Paul's advice? While the Greek text is ambiguous as is evident from the contrasted renderings, the context, however, is clearly one of remaining in the state in which a disciple was called, and so we may reasonably conclude that a slave should not take his / her freedom if it is offered.

Not all Christian slaves would be able to remain in slavery since, as noted above, the decision to free a slave rested entirely with the owner. Probably most other slaves would take the opportunity to be freedmen and freedwomen, if only to gain recognition as human beings and avoid some of the worst treatments that slaves experienced.

What would be the impact on the slave owner of a slave declining to accept manumission? Probably much the same as the Roman soldier who impressed a disciple to carry a burden for a mile and then was freely offered another mile. Similarly, if Christian slaves followed the advice regarding the correct attitude towards their masters given in the New Testament, it would have a tremendous impact because it would contrast with the more typical behaviour of slaves. Examples include:

"Servants, be obedient unto them that according to the flesh are your masters, with fear and trembling, in singleness of your heart, as unto Christ; not in the way of eyeservice, as men-pleasers; but as servants of Christ, doing the will of God from the heart; with good will doing service, as unto the Lord, and not unto men."   (Ephesians 6:5; cf Colossians 3:22)

"Let as many as are servants under the yoke count their own masters worthy of all honour, that the name of God and the doctrine be not blasphemed."   (1 Timothy 6:1)

"Exhort servants to be in subjection to their own masters, and to be well-pleasing to them in all things; not gainsaying; not purloining, but showing all good fidelity; that they may adorn the doctrine of God our Saviour in all things."

(Titus 2:9)

"Servants, be in subjection to your masters with all fear; not only to the good and gentle, but also to the froward. For this is acceptable, if for conscience toward God a man endureth griefs, suffering wrongfully."   (1 Peter 2:18)

While we are no longer subject to slavery, these principles apply today in the employer / employee relationship and may be effective in eliciting a question as to the reason for the hope within us (1 Peter 3:15), thereby affording us the privilege of witnessing for Christ.

SUMMARY

The statement regarding the possibility of accepting freedom from slavery (manumission) is ambiguous: "use it rather". Various translations render this positively, others negatively. Some versions have one possibility in the text and the opposite in the margin. The context, however, is clear: one should retain the status one had when converted and so a slave should decline freedom. This could have a significant positive impact on the slave owner's view of Christianity.

"Now concerning virgins ..."
(1 Corinthians 7:25)

I N 1 Corinthians, Paul devotes a considerable part of his letter to problems of sexual immorality that had, no doubt, arisen from the former mode of life of Gentile Corinthian converts. In Roman society no stigma attached to 'worship' involving liaisons with the 'priestesses' who served in the various temples, indeed it was commendable. However, Corinth was notorious for its gross immorality. The city had been described as the "cesspit of the Empire". Its very name had been transformed into a verb, used to describe a way of life given over wholly to debauchery and licentiousness. These factors help to explain, but not excuse, the behavioural problems which Paul had to address in his letter.

Problems at Corinth
In chapter 5 Paul deals with the problem of a form of incest which was not acceptable even in depraved pagan society, yet which the Corinthians seemed happy to tolerate (verse 1). He had previously warned them not to associate with those who participated in shameless behaviour and now he stressed that this applied particularly to anyone in the ecclesia who indulged in such things (verses 9,11). In chapter 6 he lists several perversions which had previously applied to members of the ecclesia (verses 9,10), and then deals specifically with those who continued to see nothing wrong in satisfying their sexual appetites by means of the ritual prostitution provided in the temple (verses 12-20).

In chapter 7 Paul responds to questions regarding marital relations which the Corinthians had raised in their letter to him.

For some matters he gives his personal advice (verse 12) while for others he was able to cite the commandment of the Lord (verse 10).

Those who have not yet married

Having considered issues within marriage, Paul goes on to deal with the question of "virgins", stressing that he has no specific commandment from the Lord but that he is giving advice as one who is faithful to the Lord. The problem in this passage is the identity of the "virgins". The original Greek word, παρθένος, *parthenos*, is clear enough, for it is the same as that used to describe Mary, the Lord's mother, in Matthew 1:23 and Luke 1:27. However, scholars are divided as to how the word is to be understood in this context.

Does Paul simply mean chaste unmarried women? It seems unlikely that he means this for, in the next sentence (1 Corinthians 7:26), he says that it is good for a *man* to be so, for the present distress ("crisis", NIV). There is also a masculine use of "virgin" in Revelation 14:4 which may be translated "celibate" (Phillips / Moffatt) or "chaste" (RSV / NEB).

Given the overall premise of this section of Paul's letter, namely that in the present uncertainty and the possible imminent return of the Lord Jesus (1 Corinthians 7:29) it would be prudent not to change one's status (verses 24,26), it seems most likely that Paul is dealing with those who have an option to marry or remain single, that is, those who are engaged to be married. Thiselton[1] suggests that "*those who have not married* or *those who have not yet married*" is the best description of the category rendered "virgins" as it completes the spectrum of the possible categories: married couples (verses 2-7), the widowed or separated (verses 8,9) and those contemplating separation (verses 10,11).

---

1   Thiselton, A. C. (2000) *The First Epistle to the Corinthians*, The New International Greek Testament Commentary, page 571. He notes the former matches the Greek closest but the latter the context.

In the past, and especially in Jewish circles, engagement was a much more formal arrangement than it is today. Marriage contracts were legally binding and betrothal could only be dissolved by divorce, as is evident from Joseph's predicament with Mary (Matthew 1:19). Note how Matthew writes of Joseph as Mary's "husband" and Mary as Joseph's "wife" even though they had not "come together" in marriage.

Divided loyalties?

Paul's assessment of the mindset of those who are married and those who remain single is also only really appropriate for those who still have the option to choose. The single man (1 Corinthians 7:32) is free to concentrate on his service to the Lord while the married man has additional responsibilities. There are similar pressures on the married woman in comparison to the unmarried (verse 34). Paul is concerned to ensure that those who are presently single do not find themselves under stress from divided loyalties (verse 35).

Yet Paul recognises that his advice may not be easily accepted in every case. Some of those who were engaged could find it hard to disappoint their betrothed. The phrase "behaveth … uncomely" (verse 36, KJV) cannot mean impropriety: it is "behave dishonourably", that is, a breach of promise. Paul also recognises that it would be unfair to treat a woman[2] who was 'past the bloom of youth' in this way and so diminish her future prospects of marriage. In such cases he accepts that marriage is an appropriate course of action. Similarly, Paul supports the father who consents to his engaged daughter marrying but regards his refusal as a better decision.

SUMMARY

The problem here is the use of "virgin". This is normally a chaste unmarried woman but Paul uses it of men also. It seems that here it is used of those who are unmarried but engaged to be

---

2   The Greek is not actually gender specific but it would seem a more appropriate description of a woman.

married. Paul seems to be advising that, in the present crisis (not specified), those who are single would be free from the responsibilities of married life and better able to serve the Lord. This view is advisory and Paul recognises that there are circumstances in which celibacy would be more stressful.

"A sign of power on her head, because of the angels"
(1 Corinthians 11:10)

I
T might be thought that there was little doubt as to the correct understanding of Paul's teaching in 1 Corinthians 11:4-16, namely that sisters are required to cover their heads at the breaking of bread. Yet it seems that today, in some ecclesias, this is no longer the case. This issue is not new. Garland notes: "The complexity of 11:2-16 continues to vex modern interpreters, and its comments about women rile many modern readers".[1] It is possible that some are relying on a mistaken application of verse 15:

"But if a woman have long hair, it is a glory to her: for her hair is given her for a covering."   (1 Corinthians 11:15, KJV)

Some have argued that, if she already has a covering, there is no necessity to wear anything on her head! Some commentators have concluded that Paul is dealing with the hairstyles of the period, which for a wealthy Roman woman could be very elaborate. Others have suggested that what was happening was that some women were letting their hair fall loose in the meetings and even adopting the unkempt hairstyles of the ecstatic priestesses of contemporary religions. An alternative suggestion is that sisters were taking the view that the ecclesia was a family and therefore they could literally let their hair down, or at least have their heads uncovered as at home for, normally, Roman women covered their head when they left their homes.

1   Garland, D. E. (2003) *1 Corinthians*, Baker Exegetical Commentary on the New Testament, page 505.

To go outside with their heads uncovered not only suggested that they were harlots but even if not, they could not expect the support of the law if they were attacked or molested.

Whatever the reason, the lengthy argument stresses the importance of a head covering for sisters. Paul's final comment is obviously aimed at those who cannot follow his argument – this custom is what all the other ecclesias observe:

"But if any man seemeth to be contentious, we have no such custom, neither the churches of God." (1 Corinthians 11:16)

One aspect of Paul's discourse is particularly difficult to understand:

"… for this cause ought the woman to have a sign of authority on her head, *because of the angels*."   (1 Corinthians 11:10)

What was the sign of authority? Some claim it is to signify that she is under authority, that is, having a subordinate role. The KJV translates this phrase as a sign of "power" and the margin explains, "That is, a covering, in sign that she is under the power of her husband". Not only is this a mistranslation of the Greek εξουσια, *exousia*, which means 'authority' and not 'power' (which would be δυναμις, *dunamis*), but one cannot wonder whether this was deliberate! A moment's consideration would make it evident that this marginal comment is nonsense because spinsters and widows would be free to worship bareheaded. However, the Greek *exousia* cannot be used passively, it must relate to the woman's authority. Garland[2] explains: "The head covering does not signify her subordination but her prerogative to pray and prophesy in public worship, an authority she did not formerly possess".

The correct understanding depends on the contemporary setting of Paul's remarks. Synagogues are still constructed so that women worship separately in a gallery or behind a screen. A similar arrangement obtains at the Western ('Wailing') Wall in Jerusalem. In the first ecclesia in Jerusalem, the brethren and sisters worshipped together for, after listing the apostles present, we read:

2   Garland, D. E. (2003) *loc. cit.* page 525.

"These all with one accord continued stedfastly in prayer, with the women, and Mary the mother of Jesus, and with his brethren."   (Acts 1:14)

Thus their head covering was a sign of the sisters' authority to be part of the one body. One might even say that, in Christ, the "middle wall of partition" in the synagogue had been abolished.

But what are we to make of the additional comment "... because of the angels" (1 Corinthians 11:10)? Scholarly explanations are usually unconvincing and border on the ludicrous. For example, it is said that the angels find the sight of a woman's hair erotic! One could ask why this is, if "they neither marry nor are given in marriage"? And do they not see more than this? Certainly in the Garden of Eden! Another suggestion equates the angels with the overseers of the ecclesias (equivalent to our recording and or arranging brethren today). Again, one may ask why these brethren are likely to be more susceptible than any others? Kay suggests that it is necessary that a woman "ought to have outward tokens of her subjection ... when in the church of God because of the angels who are there present, and rejoice in seeing the due order of God's creation observed".[3] Once more, we may question why only the angels need to be reassured that this is the case: would it not be an equally appropriate matter for the Lord Jesus or indeed God?

Two relevant questions should help to explain Paul's comments. Will the role of sisters differ from that of brethren in the kingdom? Will there be any gender distinction in the kingdom? Earlier in 1 Corinthians, Paul asks:

"Know ye not that the saints shall judge the world? and if the world is judged by you, are ye unworthy to judge the smallest matters? Know ye not that we shall judge angels? how much more, things that pertain to this life?"
            (1 Corinthians 6:2,3)

---

3   Kay, W. (1887) *A Commentary on the Two Epistles of St. Paul to the Corinthians*, page 45.

One must assume that this applies equally to sisters. Is Paul saying that the head covering is not only a sign of a sister's authority to attend the breaking of bread in the same room with the brethren, but a further reminder that she will have total equality in the kingdom? It is surely significant that Paul states:

> "There can be neither Jew nor Greek, there can be neither bond nor free, there can be no male and female; for ye all are one man in Christ Jesus."   (Galatians 3:28)

The RV translation includes "man" because *one* here is masculine! In John 10:30 the Lord Jesus stresses that he and the Father are one, where the Greek *hen* is neuter. Paul could have done so here but he deliberately uses the masculine *heis*. This emphasises the reality of the future, for when Paul wrote these words slaves were still slaves, even though they were the Lord's freedman (1 Corinthians 7:22); Gentiles were still Gentiles although now reckoned as Abraham's seed (Galatians 3:29). Men and women were still distinct, even in Christ, but one day they would be as the angels in heaven (Mark 12:25).

Ultimately the present differences in nationality, social status and gender will disappear. This surely is the key to this whole section. Brethren and sisters are one in Christ at the breaking of bread. This is signified by the sisters covering their hair, which is a token of their femininity to appear, figuratively, as brethren. Christ's sacrifice was as effective for women as it was for men. The head covering, which many interpret as a sign of subordination is, in fact, the indication of a sister's equality before God and a constant reminder that, in the kingdom, the present dispensational order of God, Christ, man, woman, in which the man is superior to the woman, will be abolished.

SUMMARY

The ruling that a woman should have her head covered as a sign of authority "because of the angels" has resulted in some bizarre explanations. As a sign of authority it relates to her right to sit in the ecclesial meeting with the brethren, in contrast to the Jewish synagogue convention where the women were isolated in a gallery or behind a screen. The reason "because of the angels" is more enigmatic but may relate to the future status of sisters in the kingdom where they "are equal to the angels" in the sense that gender is no longer relevant and, like the brethren, "will judge (rule) angels". It should be noted that in Paul's comment regarding the abolition of Jew / Gentile, bond / free and male / female distinctions in Christ (Galatians 3;28), he actually says that these are "one" using the masculine not neuter Greek word.

Eating the bread or drinking the cup unworthily ...

(1 Corinthians 11:27)

MANY brethren and sisters have worried about Paul's comments in 1 Corinthians 11:17-34, which superficially appear to imply that unworthiness at the Lord's table has serious implications for their eternal well-being. This phrase has been a cause of concern for many because Paul explains later in the chapter that this attitude had serious consequences for the Corinthians:

"For he that eateth and drinketh, eateth and drinketh judgment unto himself, if he discern not the body. For this cause many among you are weak and sickly, and not a few sleep."   (1 Corinthians 11:29,30)

It is possible that Paul is speaking of their spiritual health but the context seems to imply physical illness and even death.

We must first ask, 'Does anyone partake worthily of the emblems?' The answer is clearly 'No!' What the Apostle Paul seems to be addressing is the unworthy manner in which the breaking of bread meeting was conducted. This is described earlier in the chapter.

The first question is textual; what did Paul actually write? The KJV of verse 29 reads:

"For he that eateth and drinketh unworthily, eateth and drinketh damnation to himself, not discerning the Lord's body."   (1 Corinthians 11:29)

The KJV rendering may be compared with more modern translations such as the NIV and NASB:

"For anyone who eats and drinks without recognising the body of the Lord eats and drinks judgment on himself."

(1 Corinthians 11:29, NIV)

"For he who eats and drinks, eats and drinks judgment to himself, if he does not judge the body rightly."

(1 Corinthians 11:29, NASB)

In these translations the word "unworthily" is missing. This is because it was no part of the original Greek but added in the Latin tradition and then the later Medieval Greek manuscripts under the influence of verse 27:

"Wherefore whosoever shall eat the bread or drink the cup of the Lord *in an unworthy manner*, shall be guilty of the body and the blood of the Lord."   (1 Corinthians 11:27, ASV)

Even there it does not mean "unworthy" in a moral sense. This adverb means to participate at the Christian meal in a manner unworthy of the death of Christ that is here celebrated. Hence our text has not to do with eating and drinking 'unworthily' but with eating and drinking in such a way as not to be recognizing (discerning) the body. Fee[1] notes that the NIV says, "not recognizing the body *of the Lord*" while the NASB reads simply, "He does not judge the body rightly" without the words "of the Lord". This is an issue about which scholars are divided; the words are not found in any of the modern editions of the Greek text, but were derived from verse 27. It is difficult to account for the omission of these words had they been there originally. The verb *diakrino* ordinarily means to 'discern, recognize or judge rightly'.

The next issue is the identity of the "body". Is it the body of the Lord Jesus, as represented in the bread or the collective body of the believers? It is understandable that believers might refer it to the Lord's crucified body as represented in the bread, especially since the Lord specifically said, "this is (represents) my body". In verse 27 Paul says that whosoever eats and drinks in an unworthy manner is liable for the body and blood of the Lord,

---

1   Fee, G. (1987) *1 Corinthians*, The New International Commentary on the New Testament, page 558, footnote 4.

referring to their assuming the same measure of guilt as those who originally crucified Christ. However, there are two reasons for rejecting this conclusion:

1. This is the only place where the word *body* is used without qualification; elsewhere it is "my" body or the body and blood "of the Lord".

2. It is also the only instance where there is no corresponding mention of the cup or the blood.

The explanation is to be found in 10:17 where Paul explains that the bread is not only a symbol of the Lord's body but also of the ecclesial body:

"... seeing that we, who are many, are one bread, one body: for we all partake of the one bread."   (1 Corinthians 10:17)

Paul is now developing what he said earlier in this chapter. Note that he singles out the bread alone for interpretation, emphatically declaring that their partaking together of the one loaf was evidence that they themselves were therefore "one body". It should also be noted that this is the only occasion in the New Testament when the cup and bread are in that order. Paul stresses, "The bread which we break is it not the fellowship of the body of Christ?" and explains, "since there is one loaf, we who are many are one body because we partake of the one loaf". As this comment is not essential to the argument of 10:14-22 it is reasonable to suppose that it is intended to anticipate what Paul is to say here and also in chapter 12.

Fee[2] asks:

"Why therefore the absolute use of *body* in our sentence (11:29) should mean something *different* from what Paul himself says it means when *he* interprets our meal is what needs to be explained if he intended something different here ... The question is, Is this meaning for the word *body* and thus for the whole sentence supported by the context?"

---

2   Fee, G. (1996) "History as Context for Interpretation", in: *The Act of Bible Reading*, E. Dyck (Ed.), page 27.

The real issue for Paul begins at verse 17 not at verse 23, where most begin to quote this section:

> "But in giving you this charge, I praise you not, that ye come together not for the better but for the worse."
>
> (1 Corinthians 11:17)

This is a very severe criticism of the conduct of the breaking of bread for Paul is saying that it were better that they did not celebrate it at all, rather than do so in the manner that had become their custom. Paul's concern is that they are not eating the Lord's Supper (*kyriakon deipnon*) but their gathering is an *idion deipnon*, that is, a private meal taken according to the normal Roman custom. This means that their assembly was inevitably divided, not by the factions he has mentioned in 1:12 but on sociological lines:

> "... for in your eating each one taketh before other his own supper; and one is hungry, and another is drunken."
>
> (1 Corinthians 11:21)

Their behaviour at this meal was a disgrace. Some received nothing and were, as a consequence, hungry while others had consumed to excess and were drunk. They also were not 'synchronised', for some began their meal before the others and, perhaps, ate what had been prepared before the others even arrived. So Paul asks:

> "What, have ye not houses to eat and to drink in? or despise ye the church of God, and put them to shame that have not? What shall I say to you? shall I praise you? In this I praise you not."
>
> (1 Corinthians 11:22, ASV)

Paul is saying that if they want to behave like this they should do it at home. He is also angry that the richer members are humiliating those who are poor: despising the ecclesia of God by shaming the poorer members. From Paul's comments we can deduce that –

- the Corinthians celebrated the Lord's Supper as part of a regular meal and
- the way they did this destroyed the significance of the Lord's Supper because they missed the point of it, especially by the rich ignoring the needs of the poor.

In order fully to understand what was happening we need to be familiar with the normal dining customs of the time. The early churches often met in private houses[3] which, if large enough to accommodate the ecclesia, would often be in the Roman style. The rooms were arranged around an open square courtyard, the *atrium*, and the dining room, the *triclinium*, would have a three-sided table at which about a maximum of twelve could recline for their meal. This would mean that a select group would recline at the table while the remainder would be in the atrium.

The words translated 'his own supper', *to idion deipnon*, are known to be a technical term for the private meals of the well-to-do. Guests were graded so that those of the host's own social class ate near him, reclining at the *triclinium*, while the others were divided into lesser friends and his slaves or freedmen. These groups tended to have different portions and different starting times.

The ancient writers complained about this. For example, the view from the 'top table' was provided by Pliny the elder,[4] who was one of the privileged guests and was disgusted by the difference between what was provided for their host and his immediate guests and that which was given to the rest. The best dishes and wines were provided for the host and his closest friends while the remainder had to make do with cheap scraps. Similarly, three qualities of wine were placed in small flasks and allocated according to the status of the guests, the best being reserved for the host and his more important friends.

Juvenal wrote satirically and disapprovingly of this practice, giving the view from below as did Martial[5] who compared the dinner he was eating with that of his host, whose menu consisted of the finest dishes while his own was barely edible. He concluded that while he has been invited to dine with his host, they were not partaking of the same meal and, in reality, he was dining alone!

---

3   See Romans 16:3,5; 1 Corinthians 16:19; Colossians 4:15; Philemon 1,2.
4   Epistle 2.6.
5   Epigram 3.60.

It would seem possible that Paul's comment that "each one is going ahead with his own private meal" and his condemnation of the "haves" who were humiliating the "have-nots", and thereby were despising the church of God, may have been caused by something similar to the situations described by these classical authors actually occurring at the Lord's table! Could it be, for example, that at a gathering in the home of Gaius, where he and his social class were consuming their own private meal in the triclinium, the majority of those present who would mainly be drawn from the lower social orders, were being effectively excluded from the Lord's table? This regrettable disparity in social status appears to be supported by Paul's comment:

"For behold your calling, brethren, how that not many wise after the flesh, not many mighty, not many noble, are called." (1 Corinthians 1:26)

The situation in Corinth troubled Paul on two counts:

- it destroyed the meaning of the meal in which they were intended to proclaim the Lord's death until his coming; and
- the symbolic unity whereby they should have been one body, one loaf (1 Corinthians 10:17) was lost because the meal was celebrated like any other and perpetuated the old distinctions based on worldly status rather than creating a new people for God's name.

The historical context just considered is now seen to support the previous textual analysis of 1 Corinthians 11:29:

"For he that eateth and drinketh, eateth and drinketh judgment unto himself, if he discern not the body."

The body in question is not the body of the Lord Jesus (as represented in the bread) but rather the collective body of believers:

"Now ye are the body of Christ, and severally members thereof."   (1 Corinthians 12:27)

This is borne out in the reference both to eating and drinking and yet Paul makes no reference to the blood of the Lord. It is also significant that Paul uses the verb 'recognizing / discerning' with reference to the body.

The Lord's Supper is not just any meal, it is *the* meal whereby the members of his body come together in unity to declare his death. It is important to know that the description in the Greek is virtually impossible to reproduce in English because "Lord's" is not a possessive but an adjective (*kuriakon*), literally "Lordy", that is, appropriate for the Lord, for which we have no English equivalent. The same occurs in Revelation 1:10 where John was in the spirit on "the Lord's day" (*kuriake*) which, it has been suggested, can be rendered by the adjective "imperial", or something similar.

Given that this is what 1 Corinthians 11:29 means, how does it apply today? The key is unity:

"The cup of blessing which we bless, is it not a communion of the blood of Christ? The bread which we break, is it not a communion of the body of Christ? *seeing that we, who are many, are one bread, one body*: for we are all partake of the one bread."   (1 Corinthians 10:16,17)

Thus at the Lord's table we affirm that we are truly one in Christ and if not, then we are not discerning the body. Disunity at the breaking of bread destroys the whole symbolic purpose of the gathering.

SUMMARY

Paul's condemnation of the behaviour of the Corinthians at the breaking of bread appears to be a consequence of their adoption of the normal practices observed at a Roman banquet in which the guests were divided on social status. The 'top table' was occupied by the host and closest friends, whose menu and wine were superior to that of the other guests, and who usually ate first. Less important guests would dine later in another room on baser fare. The lowest ranks ate even further away and later still. Any scraps left over might be given to the slaves who had served the meal. Such behaviour at the breaking of bread destroyed its significance as a meal of unity and shamed the lowliest members of the ecclesia.

"Wherefore tongues are for a sign ..."
(1 Corinthians 14:22)

T HE full passage under consideration is:
"In the law it is written, By men of strange tongues and by the lips of strangers will I speak unto this people; and not even thus will they hear me, saith the Lord. Wherefore tongues are for a sign, not to them that believe, but to the unbelieving: but prophesying is for a sign, not to the unbelieving, but to them that believe."
(1 Corinthians 14:21,22, Phillips)

This passage may puzzle some and not others. It certainly was a problem for J. B. Phillips when he came to translate the passage in his *Letters to Young Churches*, for he reversed the accepted text so that it now read:

"That means that tongues are a sign of God's power, not for those who are unbelievers but to those who already believe. Preaching the word of God, on the other hand, is a sign of God's power to those who do not believe rather than to believers." (1 Corinthians 14:22, Phillips)

In the Preface to the twelfth edition of *Letters to Young Churches*[1] he stresses that this is the only place where he has departed from the accepted text. He continues, "I felt bound to conclude that we have here either a slip of the pen on Paul's part or a textual corruption, and I have therefore been bold enough to alter the verse in order to make good sense. One has only to read the next three verses to see the force of my alteration".

---

1   Phillips, J. B. (1947 / 1955[12]) *Letters to Young Churches*, page xv.

The problem arises from Paul's statement that tongues were a sign for unbelievers in verse 22, and then in verse 23 he appears to contradict this and continues in verse 24 to commend instead the use of prophecy as a means of converting the unbeliever. The whole section is as follows:

"Wherefore tongues are for a sign, not to them that believe, but to the unbelieving: but prophesying is for a sign, not to the unbelieving, but to them that believe. If therefore the whole church be assembled together and all speak with tongues, and there come in men unlearned or unbelieving, will they not say that ye are mad? But if all prophesy, and there come in one unbelieving or unlearned, he is reproved by all, he is judged by all; the secrets of his heart are made manifest; and so he will fall down on his face and worship God, declaring that God is among you indeed."   (1 Corinthians 14:22-25)

The Lord himself said that amongst the signs which would authenticate believers was speaking with new tongues (Mark 16:17) and this was the sign which launched the preaching at Pentecost (Acts 2:11) with remarkable results, as also occurred later in the house of Cornelius (Acts 10:46). Amongst the gifts of the Spirit, which were given in the first century "for the common good" (1 Corinthians 12:7, NIV and ESV), was speaking in tongues and their interpretation. This is in harmony with Paul's opening statement that tongues were a sign for those who were not believers.

No contradiction

Why then does Paul seem to be contradicting himself in the following verses, an apparent contradiction which convinced J. B. Phillips that there must be a textual error? If the following verses are read carefully it is evident that there is no contradiction, for Paul is clearly referring to a specific state of affairs when he states:

"If therefore the whole church be come together into *one* place, and *all* speak with tongues ..."

(1 Corinthians 14:23, KJV)

One can readily imagine the effect if everyone present at a meeting was simultaneously speaking in a range of different languages. On entering the room, an individual visitor would mostly hear a cacophony of unintelligible speech from everyone present, even if his own language was being spoken by someone, and would naturally conclude that he had stumbled into a madhouse! Even at Pentecost, some who heard the apostles speaking in tongues[2] concluded that they were inebriated.[3]

That this is the correct explanation of the apparent anomaly is confirmed by verse 27 where Paul stresses that those who are to speak in tongues be limited to two or three, and these should speak in turn:

> "If any man speaketh in a tongue, let it be by two, or at the most three, and that in turn; and let one interpret: but if there be no interpreter, let him keep silence in the church ..."
>
> (1 Corinthians 14:27,28)

On the other hand, when the assembly is engaged in prophecy, the visitor would fully understand what was being said, for verse 25 suggests that prophesying is directed towards the visitor. Similar orderliness is expected in preaching also, as Paul stresses in verses 29-31.

So, there is neither a contradiction nor any need to amend the accepted text, only that "all things be done decently and in order" (verse 40).

SUMMARY

J. B. Phillips' belief that Paul made a contradictory mistake in his treatment of the significance of speaking in tongues, and which resulted in his altering the text of 1 Corinthians 14:22, is consequence of his failure to read further to verses 23 and 24 where Paul indicates that if all spoke tongues simultaneously a

---

2   The plural "tongues" rules out the suggestion that the apostles spoke Hebrew at Pentecost.
3   These would almost certainly be those Jews who had not lived elsewhere in the Roman Empire and would not understand the languages of the countries from which the visitors came.

visitor would assume he had entered a madhouse. There is no error or contradiction in what Paul wrote.

"Baptized for the dead ..."
(1 Corinthians 15:29)

W HILE it appears that there is no consensus as to the correct understanding of this passage, and several of the suggestions are hardly satisfactory solutions to the meaning of Paul's remarks, there is general unanimity amongst commentators as to what it does not mean.

With the exception of the Mormons, who base their practice of undertaking proxy baptisms on behalf of deceased friends and relatives on this passage, no other denomination supports the view that baptism for the dead is compatible with the teaching of the rest of scripture. Equally significant is the lack of any evidence that this rite was ever practised in antiquity. Some have postulated that it might have been practised, but solely on the basis of this enigmatic comment by the Apostle Paul.

This is not one of those passages where the Greek text is difficult, as a comparison of several translations will demonstrate. A literal rendering would be:

"Otherwise what will they do [the ones] being baptized over [on behalf of] the dead [ones]? If actually dead persons are not raised, why are they then baptized over [on behalf of] them?"

The reality of resurrection
As with many difficult passages we need first to consider the context. Earlier in the chapter Paul reminds the Corinthians of the content of his preaching, which included the resurrection of

the Lord Jesus. He listed those who had seen the risen Lord – including "above five hundred brethren at once" – many being still alive and able to affirm what they had seen.

In verses 12-19, Paul is concerned to refute a dangerous corruption of the Truth which had developed in Corinth, namely the denial of the reality of resurrection. In this section he gives seven drastic consequences which follow from this particular assertion:

- Christ cannot have been raised,
- Paul's preaching has been in vain,
- The faith of the Corinthians is void,
- The apostles are false witnesses,
- The Corinthians are still in sin,
- Those who had died in faith have perished for ever,
- If the Christian hope is restricted to this life, then we are to be pitied most of all.

Paul once more affirms the reality of Christ's resurrection and relates the sequence of events leading up to the culmination of God's purpose (verses 20-28).

This puzzling passage comes as the next verse and seems at first to be an afterthought but, in reality, it extends the last of the consequences of the denial of the resurrection (verse 19). For, asks Paul, "Why stand we in jeopardy every hour?" (KJV). He then reminds his readers of his past experiences, how he faced death daily and, in particular, asks why should he risk his life if there was no prospect of resurrection, as he did in Ephesus?[1] In the absence of resurrection, his philosophy ought to be, "Let us eat and drink, for tomorrow we die".[2] Within this setting, in which Paul is stressing the reality of the resurrection and the consequences of denial, our problem passage may be explicable, at least in part.

---

1 The reference to fighting with beasts at Ephesus could be figurative but the context suggests that it could have been literal.

2 Cited from Isaiah 22:13 where Jerusalem was being fortified against the Assyrian invasion. The Lord called for appropriate solemnity on the part of the people but they celebrated in feasting, possibly because they assumed that this was their last opportunity to do so.

Kay[3] suggests there is an ellipsis[4] in this passage which may be understood as equivalent to "on behalf [of the hope] of the dead". That is, candidates for baptism affirm that they share the same belief in the resurrection as those who have died in faith. This is a similar conclusion to that of Professor Thiselton[5] who has suggested that –

"Baptism for the sake of (*huper*) the dead refers to the decision of a person or persons to ask for, and receive baptism as a result of a desire to be united with their believing relatives who have died. This presupposes that they would share the radiant confidence that they would meet again in and through Christ at the resurrection of the dead."

The significance of baptism

We may take this a little further and consider the possibility that Paul is drawing attention to the analogy between the meaning of the rite of baptism and the reality of death and resurrection. In Romans he explains that baptism is a figurative burial and resurrection (see 6:3-11). The immersion in water represents the death and burial of the old life and the surfacing again is a figurative resurrection to the new life in Christ. In seeking baptism, candidates not only affirm their belief in the necessity of the death of the old life and the raising to a new life in Christ, but also a belief in the death and resurrection of the Lord Jesus.

So, Paul may be saying that, if some Corinthians believed that those brethren and sisters who are now actually dead would never rise again, what is the point of further candidates

---

3   W. Kay (1887) *A Commentary on the Two Epistles of St. Paul to the Corinthians*, page 76.

4   Ellipsis is a very common figure of speech in which omitted words are implied or assumed in order to express the sense completely. E. W. Bullinger (1898), *Figures of Speech used in the Bible Explained and Illustrated*, gives an example from Matthew 14:19, where the Lord Jesus "gave the loaves to his disciples and the disciples to the multitude". The latter part reads literally as though the disciples were given to the multitude! However, mentally we insert the words "gave them to" so that the sense is now, "and the disciples gave them to the multitude".

5   Thiselton, A. C., *The First Letter to the Corinthians*, The New International Commentary on the Greek New Testament, page 1,248.

submitting to baptism, in which they solemnly affirm their belief in the fundamental truth which this rite symbolises? In baptism they effectively declare their belief that those who sleep in Christ will awake, so why do they submit to baptism if the whole thing is a sham?

This links in neatly with the apostle's next comment, "Why stand we in jeopardy every hour?" as though he is drawing a parallel between the pointlessness of undergoing baptism if there is no resurrection and the precarious position of those who, like Paul, had hazarded their lives in preaching a doctrine which was alleged by some Corinthians to be false.

One day, by God's grace, we may be privileged to know for certain what Paul meant, and if we are, our facility to be able to ask him will be absolute proof that the dead are raised!

SUMMARY

Baptism for the dead is practised by Mormons on the basis of 1 Corinthians 15:29. While there is no general agreement as to the meaning of Paul's words there is unanimity on the part of all others that baptism for the dead is not scriptural. Of the several suggestions as to the meaning, the most satisfactory is that the phrase is an ellipsis for "baptised on behalf [of the hope] of the dead". It is suggested that some candidates for baptism arrived at their decision because of the faith of their friends or relatives, now dead; realising that the only way they could ever meet again would be at the resurrection. Paul's point, introduced almost as an afterthought in his discourse, was that if the dead were never to rise again then those who had submitted to baptism, motivated by the example of their loved ones, had done so in vain.

"Notwithstanding she shall be saved in childbearing ..."
(1 Timothy 2:15)

S EVERAL explanations of this passage have been proposed, four of which are at least possible.[1] Most of the commentators note that much depends on the meaning of "saved" and "childbearing". It may be helpful to consider the context before attempting to see which, if any, of the options can be considered as satisfactory.

The context
Paul has been dealing with the desirable attributes of brethren and sisters. For brethren, he exhorts that they "pray every where, lifting up holy hands, without wrath and doubting" (1 Timothy 2:8).[2] His requirement for the sisters concerns their appearance and their behaviour. They should "adorn themselves in modest apparel, with shamefacedness and sobriety; not with broided hair, or gold, or pearls, or costly array". In demeanour, as is becoming for women professing godliness, they are to be occupied with good works.

Paul then deals with the relationship between men and women; especially, in context, the relationship between husband and wife: "Let the woman learn in silence with all subjection. But I suffer not a woman to teach, nor to usurp authority over the man, but to be in silence." His rationale for this obligation is found in Genesis: "For Adam was first formed, then Eve. And

1 Nicholls, A. H. (1991) *Letters to Timothy and Titus*, page 77.
2 Quotations in this chapter are from the KJV unless otherwise indicated.

Adam was not deceived, but the woman being deceived was in the transgression." The concluding comment, "Notwithstanding she shall be saved in childbearing", must relate to the preceding verses.

With this background we can now consider the various solutions which have been proposed. In attempting to understand a problem passage it often helps to reach a satisfactory solution by eliminating those explanations which are untenable.

Various solutions considered

We can begin by rejecting the idea that a sister's salvation somehow depends on bearing children, for it runs counter to all that we have revealed in scripture (e.g., Ephesians 2:8,9). It would be the worst kind of doctrine of salvation by "works"! Furthermore it would preclude unmarried sisters and others who are unable to have children. Elsewhere Paul draws attention to the spiritual merits of being single or widowed (1 Corinthians 7:32; 1 Timothy 5:5).

Some (e.g., Moffatt's translation) have simply taken the verse at face value: women will give birth safely if they "continue in faith and charity and holiness with sobriety". This is hardly satisfactory for it fails to recognise that Paul does not use 'saved' in this way: the word must have the same connotation as in 1:15 and 2:4, where it is clearly concerned with salvation in the spiritual sense. It is also not true in experience, as the cases of Rachel and the wife of Phinehas demonstrate (Genesis 35:17,18; 1 Samuel 4:19-22).

From antiquity others have noted that, since the Greek text has the definite article before "childbearing" it must refer to a particular instance. They propose that "the childbearing" is the virgin birth of the Lord Jesus. This is an attractive suggestion: it would comply with the usage of salvation by Paul, noted above, and fit the context of Genesis 3:16 to which he alludes. However, it seems to be a rather cryptic way of expressing these ideas if that is what was intended. The use of the plural "they" in 1 Timothy 2:15, implying women in general, also seems to preclude this interpretation. The principal weakness of this explanation is that Paul writes prospectively while the Lord's birth happened over half a century earlier.

An important role

There remains the explanation that it is through the woman's role of raising children that she makes her contribution to family and ecclesial life, in contrast to attempting to take on the role normally assumed by men. Paul has stressed the need for women to "learn in quietness with all subjection" (verse 11, RV); recounted his ban on women teachers and his prohibition of women having dominion (F.V) or usurping authority (KJV) over men (verse 12).

At first sight this explanation may seem somewhat inconsequential, but further consideration will show that it is in harmony with the context of his discussion of the relationship between Adam and Eve (verses 13,14). The basic idea behind the Greek verb αὐθεντεω, *authenteo*, translated "usurp authority" (KJV) is 'to domineer' or 'to act of oneself', 'to be the instigator', 'to take the initiative', 'to assume the responsibility'.[3] This was the independent role which Eve assumed and which led to her deception by the serpent.

It has been suggested that Paul emphasised childbearing because this is a distinctive feminine activity. The importance of the domestic role of sisters is evident elsewhere. For example, in chapter 5 Paul lists the many attributes which qualify a widow for ecclesial support, amongst which he includes, "if she have brought up children" (verses 9,10).

In 2:15, the word translated "childbearing", *teknogonia*, is only found here and is, therefore, not that normally used to denote the act of childbirth. Some authorities claim that it is better rendered "child-rearing".[4] In chapter 5 Paul uses a related word, *teknogoneō*. The context is relevant to our present

---

3   Nicholls, A. H. (1991) *Letters to Timothy and Titus*, page 74. It is a *hapax legomena*, that is, occurring only once.

4   See Marshall, I. H. (1999) *The Pastoral Epistles*, International Critical Commentary, page 468.

passage, for he writes: "I will therefore that the younger women marry, bear children, guide the house, give none occasion to the adversary to speak reproachfully. For some are already turned aside after Satan" (verses 14,15).

Here the task of raising children, amongst other aspects of a wife's domestic duties, is seen as a positive way of removing any grounds for complaint on the part of opponents to the Truth. Similarly, he is concerned, when writing to Titus, that the older sisters encourage the younger ones:

"... to love their husbands, to love their children, to be discreet, chaste, keepers at home, good, obedient to their own husbands, that the word of God be not blasphemed."

(Titus 2:4,5)

"Adorn the doctrine of God"

In the puzzling passage under consideration, this aspect is strengthened by Paul's addition of the words, "if they continue in faith and charity and holiness with sobriety". It is the whole demeanour of the married sisters which is important. Paul has already mentioned a dress code involving "sobriety", along with "shamefacedness" (reverence or modesty) and modesty (or decency), all of which would "adorn the doctrine of God" (Titus 2:10) rather than their person.

These attributes may not generally be appreciated in our twenty-first century culture but they are "in the sight of God of great price. For after this manner in the old time the holy women also, who trusted in God, adorned themselves, being in subjection unto their own husbands" (1 Peter 3:4,5).

The role of women in the world has changed dramatically in less than a hundred years. Some aspects of emancipation and the quest for equality are consonant with the ideals of scripture, for ultimately in Christ "there is neither male nor female". However, the efficient running of ecclesial and domestic life is facilitated by a divinely appointed division of labour which draws on the aptitudes and inclinations of men and women, husbands and wives. With infinite divine wisdom, He that "made them from the beginning made them male and female" (Matthew 19:4).

SUMMARY

Various explanations of this enigmatic phrase have been offered and four are said to be plausible. Consideration of all the evidence suggests that Paul is referring to a woman's role as a mother, trusted with the rearing of children, especially in their younger, formative years. The status of Christian women was elevated in comparison to Judaism (see chapter 28 above) and their commendable demeanour would enhance the reputation of the faith. Their specific roles, both domestically and ecclesially, are a highly significant contribution to the well-being of the community.

The "spirits in prison"
(1 Peter 3:19)

THE very phrase "spirits in prison" is puzzling. The Gnostics believed that the soul was imprisoned in the body and was released at death. In Jewish belief, however, the spirit (Hebrew, *ruach*) was the breath of life; the soul (Hebrew, *nephesh*) was the whole being, a living creature. When Adam was created, dust of the ground was animated by the breath of life (*ruach*) from God and he became a living soul (*nephesh*). At death, the breath returns to the God who gave it and the body turns again to dust (Psalm 146:4; Ecclesiastes 12:7).

The God of the spirits of all flesh
The spirit is the source of life and the phrase "God of the spirits of all flesh" stresses our dependence on Him for life. Examples in scripture include the question posed by Moses and Aaron at the rebellion of Korah:

"... O God, the God of the spirits of all flesh, shall one man sin, and wilt thou be wroth with all the congregation?"

(Numbers 16:22)

And also, at the end of his life, Moses sought that God would appoint his successor in these words:

"And Moses spake unto the LORD, saying, Let the LORD, the God of the spirits of all flesh, appoint a man over the congregation ..." (Numbers 27:15,16)

This usage suggests that the "spirits in prison" are not the disembodied 'souls' of the dead but living human beings. This is consonant with the clear Bible teaching that the dead are really dead, without consciousness:

> "For the living know that they shall die: but the dead know not anything, neither have they any more a reward; for the memory of them is forgotten. As well their love, as their hatred and their envy, is perished ... Whatsoever thy hand findeth to do, do it with thy might; for there is no work, nor device, nor knowledge, nor wisdom, in the grave, whither thou goest."   (Ecclesiastes 9:5,6,10)

Later in his letter, Peter reminds his readers of the forthcoming day of judgment noting that they –

> "... shall give account to him that is ready to judge the living and the dead. For unto this end was the gospel preached even to the dead, that they might be judged indeed according to men in the flesh, but live according to God in the spirit."
>   (1 Peter 4:5,6, ASV)

This passage includes the phrase "for unto this end was the gospel preached even unto the dead", which might be thought to counter the argument above, that the spirits in prison are not the dead.

The "living dead"

In order to understand Peter's meaning we need to consider the teaching of the Lord Jesus, who sometimes used the phrase "the dead" to indicate those who were physically alive but spiritually dead. For example, when the Lord Jesus invited someone to follow him as a disciple, the man asked to be allowed first to bury his father. If the funeral was imminent, as the Jewish custom was to bury the dead within twenty-four hours, there would be little delay. If, on the other hand, the man was saying that until his father died, and the estate was settled, he was not free to follow the Lord, by then it would probably never happen. Even pausing to say farewell to one's family was likely to result in a change of mind (Luke 9:61). In reply the Lord said: "Leave the dead to bury their own dead" (Matthew 8:22; Luke 9:60).

Again, in John's Gospel, chapter 5, the Lord refers first to those who are dead spiritually and then those who are literally dead:

> "Verily, verily, I say unto you, The hour cometh, and now is, when the dead shall hear the voice of the Son of God; and they that hear shall live. For as the Father hath life in himself, even so gave he to the Son also to have life in himself."
>
> (John 5:25)

His remark "and now is" denotes the current preaching activity. He goes on to say:

> "Marvel not at this: for the hour cometh, in which all that are in the tombs shall hear his voice, and shall come forth ..."
>
> (John 5:28,29)

This indicates that those who are literally dead will hear his voice on the day of resurrection by the reference to "all who are dead".

Spirits in prison

From the above, it seems possible that the phrase "spirits in prison" is a reference to those who are alive physically but are dead spiritually because they are imprisoned by sin and therefore facing the 'death penalty' as a consequence. In the synagogue at Nazareth, the Lord Jesus read Isaiah 61, indicating that it prophesied his own work:

> "And there was delivered unto him the book of the prophet Isaiah. And he opened the book, and found the place where it was written, The Spirit of the Lord is upon me, because he anointed me to preach good tidings to the poor: he hath sent me to proclaim release to the captives, and recovering of sight to the blind, to set at liberty them that are bruised, to proclaim the acceptable year of the Lord. And he closed the book, and gave it back to the attendant, and sat down: and the eyes of all in the synagogue were fastened on him. And he began to say unto them, Today hath this scripture been fulfilled in your ears."   (Luke 4:17-21)

His work was to preach good tidings, the Gospel, and release the captives, setting them at liberty, that is, "the spirits in prison".

The latter was accomplished by his own suffering, "being put to death in the flesh, but quickened (made alive again) by the Spirit". It was in the power of the Holy Spirit that he preached and performed miracles (Luke 4:14).

The days of Noah

The real difficulty in understanding this passage is the comment in 1 Peter 3:19,20, which seems to imply that Christ preached 'in (or by) the (Holy) spirit' that 'quickened him', back in the days of Noah. This may appear to support the 'pre-existence' of Christ, a self-contradictory term in itself, but further analysis shows that this cannot be correct. Christ's 'quickening' was after his death and so only 'time travel' would allow a retrospective involvement with the population in Noah's day. It is possible that "he" in this content is God, because this is the antecedent in verse 18 and the "longsuffering of God" is mentioned in verse 20. Peter mentions the days of Noah twice in his second letter (2 Peter 2:5; 3:6), but without any reference to the personal involvement of Christ.

One ingenious suggestion, by Dr. Rendel Harris, that the Greek phrase ’εν ‘ω και, *en hō kai*, 'in which indeed', should be ’Ενωχ, *Enoch* who prophesied in a degenerate age (Jude 14).

This rendering has been adopted in the Goodspeed and Moffatt versions. Moffatt provides an explanatory footnote.[1] This proposed amendment of the text indicates how difficult this passage is regarded even by those who embrace conventional false doctrines.

The spirit of Christ

Peter provides us with the correct understanding of this 'puzzling passage' in the opening chapter of his letter, where he contrasts the present problems of his readers with the coming salvation that they anticipate in faith:

---

1   "Accepting the emendation of Dr. Rendel Harris that ’Ενωχ has been omitted after ’εν ‘ω και (ΕΝΩΚΑΙ [ΕΝΩΧ]), by 'a scribe's blunder in dropping some repeated letters'."

"Concerning which salvation the prophets sought and searched diligently, who prophesied of the grace that should come unto you: searching what time or what manner of time the Spirit of Christ which was in them did point unto, when it testified beforehand the sufferings of Christ, and the glories that should follow them."   (1 Peter 1:10,11)

Peter indicates that the prophets of old were privileged to have revealed to them the purpose of God in Christ from the very beginning. This is called the "Spirit of Christ" because it concerned Christ, the central part of God's purpose, "the eternal purpose [or purpose of the ages] which He purposed in Christ Jesus our Lord" (Ephesians 3:11).

Peter actually stresses this in his first chapter:

"... Christ: who was foreknown indeed before the foundation of the world, but was manifested at the end of times for your sake ..."   (1 Peter 1:19,20)

Enoch prophesied of the coming of the Lord (Jude 14), Abraham rejoiced to see the Lord's day (John 8:56), David knew of the promise made by the Lord God to his Lord, who would also be his descendant (Psalm 110:1; Matthew 22:44; etc.).

Noah was a prophet (Genesis 9:25-27) and so we assume that he would be included in Peter's comment. Noah was "a preacher of righteousness" (2 Peter 2:5) and although we are not told the content of his message, we know that he "condemned the world" of his time (Hebrews 11:7). Yet it would surely not be only a negative message, for in our own preaching we proclaim the positive message of salvation in Christ and the coming kingdom. The duration of his preaching would be significant: "when the longsuffering of God waited in the days of Noah" (1 Peter 3:20).

The spirits of just men made perfect

The puzzle is solved. The spirits locked in their prison of sin did not respond to the preaching of Noah and so perished. Peter compares the waters that supported the ark and saved Noah and his family with the waters of baptism that save the faithful.

Imprisoned spirits are released and ultimately made perfect. In the words of the writer of Hebrews:

> "... ye are come unto mount Zion, and unto the city of the living God, the heavenly Jerusalem, and to innumerable hosts of angels, to the general assembly and church of the firstborn who are enrolled in heaven, and to God the Judge of all, and to the spirits of just men made perfect, and to Jesus the mediator of a new covenant."   (Hebrews 12:22-24)

SUMMARY

The phrase "spirits in prison" does not refer to disembodied souls locked away until judgement or souls imprisoned in mortal bodies. Rather it refers to those who are alive physically but dead spiritually, being imprisoned by sin and, consequently awaiting the 'death penalty'. Those in the days of Noah (1 Peter 3:19,20) did not respond to preaching and so perished. Peter compares the waters of the Flood that saved Noah and his family with the waters of baptism that save the faithful. Imprisoned spirits are released and ultimately made perfect (Hebrews 12:23).

"The angels that kept not their first estate"

(Jude 6; 2 Peter 2)

THE two puzzling passages for consideration are:
"And angels which kept not their own principality, but left their proper habitation, he hath kept in everlasting bonds under darkness unto the judgment of the great day. Even as Sodom and Gomorrah, and the cities about them ... in like manner ..." (Jude 6,7)
"For if God spared not angels when they sinned, but cast them down to hell, and committed them to pits of darkness, to be reserved unto judgment; and spared not the ancient world, but preserved Noah ..." (2 Peter 2:4,5)

Given the close similarities between Jude and 2 Peter, it seems reasonable to assume that these quotations are describing the same event. The two passages include "angels", "darkness" and also "judgment" as a consequence of their actions. They also have in common an associated historical event that involves the destruction of the wicked, one by a flood, the other by a conflagration. In the larger context of both passages, with the possible exception of these "angels", the other entities are all human. They are also concerned with the destruction of a large majority and the saving of a remnant. In Jude we have the Exodus, in which the majority of those who left Egypt perished in the wilderness, and the destruction of Sodom which destroyed all but Lot and his two daughters. In Peter we have the Flood from which only eight survived and Sodom and Gomorrah with three.

While the identity of these angels is the principal puzzle, it seems that they are part of the history recorded in the Old Testament. It is helpful at this stage to ask whether these 'angels' are part of the innumerable angelic host whose characteristics are described in scripture. The attributes of angels may be summarised as follows:

- They are supernatural (Mark 13:32; Hebrews 2:7), powerful (Psalm 103:20; 2 Thessalonians 1:7) immortal beings (Luke 20:36).
- They act as God's agents (Genesis 3:24; 16:7; 19:12,13; 2 Samuel 24:16; Isaiah 37:36; Acts 12:23).
- They are at work on earth (Hebrews 1:14), acting on behalf of God's people (Psalm 34:7; Matthew 18:10).

These facts suggest that the "angels" of these puzzling passages are not the same as those found widely in scripture. It is significant that, in Revelation chapters 2 and 3, letters are written to the "angels" of seven ecclesias. Although Revelation is given to John by the Lord Jesus through the mediation of an angel, John writes to them (Revelation 1:4) and is instructed also to write to them in 1:19. It would be rather odd for the angel to tell John to write to seven other angels! If, however, these seven "angels" are human this would be more appropriate. In the organisation of the synagogue, there was the Ruler of the Synagogue (Luke 8:41; Acts 13:15; 18:8,17) who was in charge of the affairs and regulated the services and also the *Sh^eliach* (or *mal'ak*) *hazzibor*, equivalent to the angel of the ecclesia.[1] Having established that 'angels' can be human we may now attempt to identify an Old Testament incident that involves pits of darkness and judgement.

One incident seems to meet these requirements: the rebellion of Korah, Dathan and Abiram. It began with "despising dignities":

"Now Korah, the son of Izhar, the son of Kohath, the son of Levi, with Dathan and Abiram, the sons of Eliab, and On,

---

1   Bullinger, E.W., *The Companion Bible*, Appendix 120, page 159.

the son of Peleth, sons of Reuben, took men: and they rose up before Moses, with certain of the children of Israel, two hundred and fifty princes of the congregation, called to the assembly, men of renown; and they assembled themselves together against Moses and against Aaron, and said unto them, Ye take too much upon you, seeing all the congregation are holy, every one of them, and the LORD is among them: wherefore then lift ye up yourselves above the assembly of the LORD?"   (Numbers 16:1-3)

Moses was, quite naturally, offended by this accusation, for he had not sought his office, indeed he had reluctantly accepted it at the burning bush. It must have been revealed to him that the Lord would demonstrate that Moses' position was divinely appointed and that incontrovertible evidence of this choice would be provided. The following day the company of rebels were to take censers, put fire into them and offer incense. God would then indicate His choice. Moses concluded by accusing these Levites of too much self-importance and especially of despising the special office to which they had been appointed and aspiring, it seemed, to the priesthood. As had happened so often in the past, there was criticism of Moses for not bringing them into a land flowing with milk and honey but only a wilderness. It is a common experience that once complaints are launched, all other grievances come to the surface also. Moses rebutted these accusations and set out the procedure for the test of divine approval.

The next day the rebels assembled with their censers, put fire in them and added the incense. They then assembled at the door of the tabernacle. The glory of God appeared and Moses and Aaron were commanded to keep their distance from the whole congregation because it was about to be destroyed in a moment. Moses and Aaron besought the Lord that the whole people should not perish for the sin of Korah and He relented. The whole congregation was then warned that they should distance themselves from the rebels lest they too be consumed.

In words reminiscent of those used by the Lord Jesus in John 5:30, Moses now stressed that he had been commissioned by God "to do all these works; for" he said, "I have *not* done them of mine own mind" and continued by emphasising that if these men died a normal death "then the LORD hath not sent me" (Numbers 16:28,29). This would be the test whereby it would become evident that he had not taken too much upon him.

The test of who was approved by God was to be quite simple but unusual: if the rebels died of something familiar, then Moses was the usurper, but if their death was extraordinary, this would vindicate Moses. What is certain is that they would die for their sin:

> "If these men die the common death of all men, or if they be visited after the visitation of all men; then the LORD hath not sent me. But if the LORD make a new thing, and the ground open her mouth, and swallow them up, with all that appertain unto them, and they go down alive into the pit (margin: "Heb. *Sheol*"); then ye shall understand that these men have despised the LORD."   (Numbers 16:29,30)

Moses had hardly finished his explanation when the ground opened and they were swallowed up alive going down into Sheol as Moses indicated. The use of the word "pit" in Numbers 16:30,33, matches the phrase "pits of darkness" in 2 Peter 2:4.

These rebels are now being "kept in everlasting bonds under darkness unto the judgment of the great day" (Jude) and God has "committed them to pits of darkness, to be reserved unto judgment" (Peter).

SUMMARY

The "angels" here are human in the sense in which the word is used in Revelation chapters 2 and 3. They did not keep their original status because Korah, Dathan and Abiram rebelled in the time of Moses and were swallowed up by the earth, to be "kept in everlasting bonds" (Jude) and committed to "pits of darkness" (2 Peter), reserved for judgement.

The dispute over the body of Moses
(Jude 9)

> "But Michael the archangel, when contending with the devil he disputed about the body of Moses, durst not bring against him a railing judgement, but said, The Lord rebuke thee."
>
> (Jude 9)

IT has been generally assumed that this passage is a quotation from the apocryphal book *The Assumption of Moses* (also known as *The Testament of Moses*). Bauckham[1] has noted that –

> "Although the source of Jude's story of the dispute over the body of Moses is not extant, a wealth of material is available from which it should be possible to reconstruct the story which Jude knew."

In fact, not only is the relevant part of the book missing, but there is no certainty that it ever existed and certainly not in Jude's time. It has been suggested that the "missing" book had to be concocted on the basis of Jude's alleged extract!

It is pertinent to ask why the conventional devil, a supernatural being, should want to have the body of Moses? One would expect that the devil of common perception would be more interested to acquire his (immortal) soul! The word translated "devil" in Jude is the Greek διαβολος, *diabolos*, slanderer or false accuser. It is significant that the word 'devil' does not occur in the Old Testament. It is commonly assumed that the Hebrew word 'satan' is the Old Testament equivalent but this is not correct, for

---

1   Bauckham, R. J. (1983) *Jude, 2 Peter*, Word Biblical Commentary 50, page 65.

the Hebrew word is neutral, meaning 'adversary'. It can denote adversaries for good (cf. the angel in Numbers 22:22) as well as for evil. These factors alone should suggest that the passage cannot be understood other than in Biblical terms and this must be borne in mind throughout any exegesis of the passage.

Jude makes allusions to several incidents recorded in the Old Testament, such as the Exodus (verse 5); the overthrow of Sodom and Gomorrah (verse 7); Cain, Balaam and Korah (verse 11). The allusion to "angels which kept not their own principality" and this passage in verse 9 are cryptically recounted but, as a working hypothesis, it is reasonable to suppose that these are also references to incidents recorded in the Old Testament.

Two phrases in Jude appear to have links with Zechariah 3:

Jude	Zechariah 3:2
"But Michael the archangel, when contending with the devil he disputed about the body of Moses, durst not bring against him a railing judgement, but said, *The Lord rebuke thee*." (verse 9)	"And the LORD said unto Satan, *The LORD rebuke thee*, O Satan ..."
"and some save, *snatching them out of the fire*; and on some have mercy with fear; hating even the garment spotted by the flesh." (verse 23)	"... the LORD that hath chosen Jerusalem rebuke thee: is not this a brand *plucked out of the fire*?"

As noted above, 'devil' is not an Old Testament word, but it is evident in comparing these two passages that Satan in Zechariah 3:2 is the Old Testament equivalent here. Furthermore, there are grounds for believing that Jude was influenced by 2 Peter, as the comparison in the table overleaf demonstrates.

Peter's account is quite evidently concerned with human behaviour in contrast to that of angels. These are evil men who slander others (that is, they are 'devils', literally 'false accusers') in their self-important ignorance and are doomed to destruction. It follows that the passage in Jude must also be concerned with human adversaries (satans) of similar character.

Jude	2 Peter 2 and 3
"Yet in like manner these also in their dreamings *defile* the *flesh*, and *set at nought dominion*, and *rail at dignities*." (verse 8)	"But chiefly them that walk after the *flesh* in the lust of *defilement*, and *despise dominion*. Daring, self-willed, they tremble not to *rail at dignities*." (2:10)
"But Michael the *archangel*, when contending with the devil he disputed about the body of Moses, durst not bring against him a *railing judgement*, but said, *The Lord* rebuke thee." (verse 9)	"Whereas *angels*, though greater in might and power, bring not a *railing judgement* against them before *the Lord*." (2:11)
"But ye, beloved, *remember ye the words which have been spoken before by* the *apostles* of our *Lord* Jesus Christ." (verse 17)	"That ye should *remember the words which were spoken before by* the holy prophets, and the commandments of the *Lord* and Saviour through your *apostles*." (3:2)
"That they said to you, *In the last time there shall be mockers, walking after their own* ungodly *lusts*." (verse 18)	"Knowing this first, *that in the last days mockers shall come with mockery, walking after their own lusts*." (3:3)

Returning to the passage in Zechariah, it probably relates to the period of the return from exile when the priests were deposed from office because of inadequate genealogical qualifications:

"And from among the priests ... These searched for their family records, but they could not find them and so were excluded from the priesthood as unclean. The governor ordered them not to eat any of the most sacred food until there was a priest ministering with the Urim and Thummim."

(Ezra 2:61-63, NIV)

It seems likely that these men complained that the High Priest, Joshua, should also be disqualified since he no longer had access to the high-priestly robes, which, no doubt disappeared during the Babylonian captivity. God answered their complaint through His prophet, Zechariah:

"Then he showed me Joshua the high priest standing before the angel of the LORD, and Satan standing at his right side to accuse him. The LORD said to Satan, 'The LORD rebuke you, Satan! The LORD, who has chosen Jerusalem, rebuke you! Is not this man a burning stick snatched from the fire?' Now Joshua was dressed in filthy clothes as he stood before the angel. The angel said to those who were standing before him, 'Take off his filthy clothes.' Then he said to Joshua, 'See, I have taken away your sin, and I will put rich garments on you.' Then I said, 'Put a clean turban on his head.' So they put a clean turban on his head and clothed him, while the angel of the LORD stood by."   (Zechariah 3:1-5, NIV)

We have a parallel with Jesus (Joshua). He too was rejected and despised by Israel's leaders, who repeatedly falsely accused him during his ministry (i.e., were 'devils') and at his trial before Pilate, even though he was declared to be God's High Priest (cf. Hebrews 3:1,2; 4:14-16). In due course, their rejection of him became the cause of their own rejection by God. The Lord Jesus did not condemn the Jewish rulers but committed his cause to God –

"... who, when he was reviled, reviled not again; when he suffered, he threatened not; but committed himself to him that judgeth righteously ..."   (1 Peter 2:23, KJV)

Jude is dealing with a similar situation, where those who are attempting to corrupt the faith are behaving just like those in Zechariah's day, and are therefore subject to divine judgement.

The body of Moses

There remains the enigmatic use of the phrase, "the body of Moses". It has been argued that this is the Old Testament counterpart of the body of Christ (Ephesians 1:23; 1 Corinthians 12:27) and represents the children of Israel who were baptized into Moses and in the sea (1 Corinthians 10:1,2). It is interesting to note that Ephesians 2:16 (RV) says that Christ reconciled both Jews and Gentiles into *one* body and may detract from this explanation. The view that "the body of Moses" is Israel, however, is not found in scripture and it does not fit the context of Zechariah 3.

The word for body (Greek σομα, *soma*) does not necessarily mean a *dead* body and furthermore it is used elsewhere for a slave or bondservant, who was regarded in New Testament times not as a human being but as a thing, a chattel, a body to be used. The word is used in this way in Revelation 18:13 as is evident when comparing the KJV and NIV renderings of this passage.

Revelation 18:13 (KJV)	Revelation 18:13 (NIV)
"And cinnamon, and odours, and ointments, and frankincense, and wine, and oil, and fine flour, and wheat, and beasts, and sheep, and horses, and chariots, and *slaves*, and souls of men."	"... cargoes of cinnamon and spice, of incense, myrrh and frankincense, of wine and olive oil, of fine flour and wheat; cattle and sheep; horses and carriages; and *bodies* and souls of men."

This fits the context quite well. The first Joshua (Jesus) was literally the servant (slave, body) of Moses (Exodus 24:13) and the Joshua of Zechariah 3 was a dedicated servant (slave, body) of Moses through the Law.

SUMMARY

The claimed parallel between of "the body of Christ" as a collective description of believers and "the body of Moses" as Israel does not appear to have scriptural support. The use of "body" in the New Testament for slaves (Revelation 18:13) may apply here. It would then fit well with the fact that the first Joshua was the literal servant of Moses and Joshua, the High Priest of Zechariah 3, also was a dedicated servant (slave) of Moses through the Law.

Bibliography

Abel, R. (2011[2]) *Wrested Scriptures, A Christadelphian Handbook of Suggested Explanations to Difficult Bible Passages*, Revised and Expanded by J. Allfree, The Christadelphian, Birmingham, xvi + 399 pages.

Barclay, W. (1968) *The New Testament, A New Translation*, Volume 1, Collins, London, 352 pages.

Bartchy, S. S. (1992) "Slavery (Greco-Roman)", in: *The Anchor Bible Dictionary*, D. N. Freedman (Ed.), Doubleday, New York, Vol. 6, pages 65-73.

Bauckham, R. J. (1983) *Jude, 2 Peter*, Word Biblical Commentary Volume 50, D. A. Hubbard & G. W. Barker (Eds.), Word Books, Waco, xix + 357 pages.

Bernard, J. H. (1928) *A Critical and Exegetical Commentary on the Gospel according to St. John*, The International Critical Commentary, A. H. McNiele (Ed.), T. & T. Clark, Edinburgh, 2 volumes, clxxxviii + 740 pages.

Brown, R. E. (1971) *The Gospel According to John, Volume 1, I-XII*, The Anchor Bible, W. F. Albright & D. N. Freedman (Eds.), Geoffrey Chapman, London, cxlvi + 538 pages.

Bruce, F. F. (1983) *The Gospel of John, Introduction, Exposition and Notes*, William B. Eerdmans Publishing Company, Grand Rapids, xi + 425 pages.

Bruce, F. F. (1983) *The Hard Sayings of Jesus*, The Jesus Library, M. Green (Ed.), Hodder and Stoughton, London, 267 pages.

Brunt, P. A. (1987) "Labour", in: *The Roman World, Vol. II*, J. Wacher (Ed.), Routledge & Kegan Paul Ltd., London, xiv + pages 481-872.

Bullinger, E. W. (1894 / 1967[Reprint]) *Number in Scripture, Its Supernatural Design and Spiritual Significance*, Kregel Publications, Grand Rapids, vii + 303 pages.

Bullinger, E. W. (1898 / 1968[Reprint]) *Figures of Speech used in the Bible Explained and Illustrated*, Baker Book House, Grand Rapids, xlvii + 1,104 pages.

Carson, D. A. (1991) *The Gospel According to John*, The Pillar New Testament Commentary, D. A. Carson (Ed.), Apollos, Nottingham / William B. Eerdmans, Grand Rapids / Cambridge UK, 715 pages.

Cassuto, U. (1961) *A Commentary on the Book of Genesis, Part I From Adam to Noah, A Commentary on Genesis 1-VI8*, The Magnes Press, The Hebrew University, Jerusalem, xviii + 323 pages.

Cox, P. (2013) "153 Fishes", *Testimony*, Vol. 83, No. 984, July 2013, page 277.

Fee, G. D. (1987) *The First Epistle to the Corinthians*, The New International Commentary on the New Testament, F. F. Bruce (Ed.), William B. Eerdmans Publishing Company, Grand Rapids, xxiv + 880 pages.

Fee, G. D. (1996) "History as Context for Interpretation", in: *The Act of Bible Reading*, E. Dyck (Ed.), InterVarsity Press, Downers Grove, 182 pages.

Garland, D. E. (2003) *1 Corinthians*, Baker Exegetical Commentary on the New Testament, R. W. Yarborough & R. H. Stein (Eds.), Baker Academic, Grand Rapids, xxi + 870 pages.

Guilding, Aileen (1960) *The Fourth Gospel and Jewish Worship, A study of the relation of St. John's Gospel to the ancient Jewish lectionary system*, Oxford University Press, London, 247 pages.

Harrison, R. K. (1990) *Numbers*, The Wycliffe Exegetical Commentary, K. L. Barker (Ed.), Moody Press, Chicago, xvi + 452 pages.

Hellawell, J. M. (2014) *Beginning at Jerusalem ... The Growth of the Gospel Message in the Acts of the Apostles*, The Christadelphian, Birmingham, xvii + 397 pages.

Hunter, A. M. (1965) *The Gospel according to John*, The Cambridge Bible Commentary on the New English Bible, P. R. Ackroyd, A. R. C. Leaney & J. W. Packer (Eds.), Cambridge University Press, Cambridge, ix + 205 pages.

Josephus, F. (1963^{Reprint}) *Complete Works*, Translated by W. Whiston, Kregel Publications, Grand Rapids, xxi + 770 pages.

Kay, W. (1887) *A Commentary on the Two Epistles of St. Paul to the Corinthians*, MacMillan and Co., London, vii + 146 pages.

Lewis, R. (2014) *Abraham and Sarah*, The Christadelphian, Birmingham, viii + 246 pages.

Mare, W. H. (1976) *1 Corinthians*, The Expositor's Bible Commentary, Vol. 10, F. E. Gaebelein (Ed.), The Zondervan Corporation, Grand Rapids, xvi + 508 pages.

Marshall, I. H. (1999) *The Pastoral Epistles*, The International Critical Commentary, J. A. Emerton, C. E. B. Cranfield and G. N. Stanton (Eds.), T. & T. Clark International, London, xlii + 869 pages.

Metzger, B.M. (1994^2) *A Textual Commentary on the Greek New Testament, A companion Volume to the United Bible Societies' Greek New Testament (Fourth Revised Edition)*, Deutsche Bibelgesellschaft / United Bible Societies, Stuttgart / New York, xiv + 696 pages.

Milne, B. (1993) *The Message of John, Here is your King!* The Bible Speaks Today, New Testament, J. Stott (Ed.), Inter-Varsity Press, Leicester, 352 pages.

Nicholls, A. (1991) *Letters to Timothy and Titus, Sound Words for Ecclesias under Pressure*, The Christadelphian, Birmingham, x + 438 pages.

Owen, P. (2013) "153 Fishes", *Testimony*, Vol. 83, No. 981, March 2013, page 98.

Phillips, J. B. (1947 / 1955[12]) *Letters to Young Churches, A Translation of the New Testament Epistles*, Geoffrey Bles Ltd., London, xv + 224 pages.

Phillips, J. B. (1959[2]) "Foreword", in: Marshall, A. D., *The Interlinear Greek-English New Testament*, Samuel Bagster & Sons Limited, London, xviii + 1,027 pages.

Simons, A. (2014) "153 Fishes", *Testimony*, Vol. 84, No. 993, April 2014, page 147.

Thiselton, A. C. (2000) *The First Epistle to the Corinthians, A Commentary on the Greek Text*, I. H. Marshall & D. A. Hagner (Eds.), The New International Greek Testament Commentary, William B. Eerdmans Publishing Company, Grand Rapids / The Paternoster Press, Carlisle, xxxiii + 1,446 pages.

Watkins, P. (No date) *Some Difficult Passages*, four volumes, The Christadelphian Isolation League.

Wenham, G. J. (1987) *Genesis 1-15*, Word Biblical Commentary, Word Books, Waco, liii + 353 pages.

Wescott, B. F. (1880 / 1958) *The Gospel of St. John, The Authorized Version with Introduction and Notes, and a new Introduction by A. Fox*, James Clark & Co., Ltd, London, iii + xcvii + 307 pages.

Whittaker, H. A. (1966/1989[2]) *Abraham: Father of the Faithful*, The Christadelphian, Birmingham, vi + 114 pages.

Whittaker, H. A. (1969) *He is Risen Indeed*, self-publication, vi + 117 pages.

Whittaker, H. A. (1987) *Israel in the Wilderness*, Biblia, Cannock, vi + 185 pages.

Whittaker, H. A. (1984 / 1989[2]) *Studies in the Gospels, A New Extended Edition*, Biblia, Cannock, xiv + 863 pages.

Whittaker, H. A. (1989) *Studies in the Books of Judges and Ruth*, Biblia, Cannock, vii + 251 pages.

Whittaker, H. A. (1995) *A Look at those "Difficult" Passages*, Printland Publishers, Hyderabad, India, 81 pages.

Young, R. (1879 / 1939[8]) *Analytical Concordance to the Holy Bible*, Lutterworth Press, London, xii + 1,262 pages.

Scripture index

Topical index